Ilanu Tashken Chodjond

Kokain Kashgar

Khara Aderkand

Sumerkund

R.Jihon Koi Hissar Basskhed Ourting Yarkand

Balkh L.Tus R.Yo

Zundee Hindoo Koosh Hoondooz LITTLE BHARIA Desert CH

Caubul Ghuznee Chingles Jellabad Laidak Mt. Guinnak Hourka

CAUBUL Kandahar Indus Cashmere Chowdburre Kinchah L.Terkiri

AFGHANISTAN Lound Mondtaa Attock Dhooti Gortope Sera

Khoosly Lill Lahore PUNJAB THIBET Tchangaprong Lassa

Morades Guadava Bhawulpore Himalaya Mts Palte

Aba Sin & Ootch Bhutnair Delhi Bareilly NEPAUL Goorcha BHOTAN

Bikanair Jodpoor Bhurtpoor Agra Biswah Ghattanda

Hyvrabad Ajmere Kerowl Evzabad Oude Benares Bettiah Dinagepore

SINDE Tattah Loony R Gwalior Ditteah Allahabad Moorshedabad

Bhooj Oodipoor Boondee Kotah Patna BENGAL Nagere

Kutch Ahmedabad HINDOSTAN Ougein Belhari Burdee Calcutta

GHUJERAT Oana Nerbuddah R. Deoghur Ruttumpoor Mouths of the Ganges

G.of Cambay DECCAN Booarumpoor Nagpoor Belaspoor Arracan

Soorut Boornair Boodah Cuttack Ram

Demaun Aurungabad Choomory ORISSA

Bombay Ahmednuggur Chindor Godavery Gurjoan

Ft.Victoria Briapore Golconda Ciracole

Davour Beder Hyderabad Rajamandry Ch

Goa Raichore Kistnah R Nizampatam BENGAL Dal

Munly Nuggur Onoole C.

Chittelroog

The Sky Above,
The Kingdom Below

The Sky Above,
The Kingdom Below

In the Footsteps of Thomas Coryate

by
Daniel Allen

 ArmchairTraveller

HAUS PUBLISHING
London

Copyright © 2008 Daniel Allen

First published in Great Britain in 2008 by Haus Publishing Ltd,
26 Cadogan Court, Draycott Avenue, London SW3 3BX
www.hauspublishing.co.uk

The moral rights of the author have been asserted.

A CIP catalogue record for this book is available from the British
Library

ISBN 978-1-905791-30-9

Typeset in Garamond 3 by MacGuru Ltd
Printed and bound in India by International Print-o-Pac Limited
Jacket illustration: Getty Images

Contents

Acknowledgements   ix

Prologue: The Tomb Beneath the Sky   1

Part I: **Syria, Turkey and the Ottoman Empire**   7
Chapter 1: Damascus: Roses and Refuse   9
Chapter 2: Hama Horror   33
Chapter 3: The Renaissance in the Wilderness   59
Chapter 4: Armenia the Lesser   83

Part II: **Persia and the Safavid Empire**   101
Chapter 5: Dressing Up   105
Chapter 6: Half the World   129
Chapter 7: The Desert Prophet   157

Part III: **India, Pakistan and
       the Mughal Empire**   185
Chapter 8: Chaos by Consent   189
Chapter 9: The Long Walk   213
Chapter 10: The Truth Beneath the Tomb   237

Epilogue   255
Bibliography   257

For my family
With love

Acknowledgements

For assistance along the way I would like to thank Mahmood Allwash, Said al-Sharf, Bita Irandoost, Omid Karimi, Ashkan Azarmi, Arselan Azarmi, Zohreh Shirani, Shabti Ahmad, and especially Joel Wellington Christie. My thanks also to Christine King and Jamie Savan; and for less direct, though no less valuable, help: Fernando Azocar, Anna Etoray, Stijn Oosterling, Paul P W Kwon, Pauline Eckerström, Tim Frodsham, Alison Maxwell. And in Estonia Eva Tolouze and the Remmel family, Tiina Sepp and Madli Kütt.

I would also like to thank Nicholas Shakespeare for his advice in the early stages of this project. Finally many thanks to Sheila Ableman, who saw a book in the idea I proposed, and to Anne Joseph who helped it see daylight.

Note

The journey portrayed in this book took place between May 2004 and January 2005. The majority of names have been changed.

Seventeenth-century spelling and grammar can be considerably different from that of today. I have tried to stick to the original where possible and made changes only if it was necessary for clarity.

After publishing *Coryat's Crudities*, Coryate added an e to his name. I have preserved the two spellings in the text.

Prologue

The Tomb Beneath the Sky

At the village of Suvali the sky is bleached to a pale blue by the sea. On the wide beach an occasional palm serves to emphasise the flatness of the landscape. Tangled, scrappy vegetation grows in handfuls in the sand. Nearby, the warm waters of the Gulf of Cambay, the north-eastern corner of the Arabian Sea, drop exhausted onto the shore with nothing more than a sigh and a gurgle. Out here where the land dissolves into the sea, the world is all sky.

The road begins at Suvali and runs east inland. In the hamlet of Rajgiri a mile away, the scrub is well established. Thorns are like barbed wire here, so strong they pierce the soles of shoes, dense enough to be used as fencing. The place is nothing more than a couple of stone villas silhouetted against the light.

Close to where I stand three water buffalo tethered beneath a coarse tree shift lazily in the warm winter sun. Dust furls in the breeze, rising like exhaust from the landscape. Overhead a kite is poised, crying and wheeling against the air.

On a low sandy hill in front of me an old Mughal monument stands fast. It is a simple building of four clustered columns and a small cupola, dirty now with pollution though still with traces of red paint. The dome's stone lantern was cracked in the Gujarat earthquake of 2001 and the top portion has broken away.

From 30 yards – the furthest I can back away in the thorny scrub – the proportions are pleasing. The monument is unornamented, perhaps 30 feet tall and 15 feet across. It is a self-contained little place, and small enough to be almost completely forgotten on this sandy littoral just ten miles from Surat, a city of four million. The few people who do remember the building know it as 'Tom Coryate's Tomb', a monument to one of the most extraordinary Englishmen who ever lived, and my journey's end.

～

In his time – the early 1600s – Thomas Coryate was known as a great traveller, a writer, a wit, a member of the royal household and a friend to the great and good. Coryate was introduced to London society in the first few years of the reign of James I and became a regular visitor to the court of his precocious son Henry, Prince of Wales. Here he performed a role not unlike that of a court jester, earning a name for himself as a 'learned buffoon' with his act, a mish-mash of overblown monologue and comical concocted Latin, as was the fashion of the day. But Coryate's comedy was underpinned by a sharp brain. There were few at court who could beat him in a duel of wits, even when the guests included such luminaries as John Donne, Ben Jonson and Inigo Jones.

In addition to his court life Coryate also had a defining passion for travel. In 1608 he spent five months exploring Europe in a groundbreaking journey that would win him a place in history. He walked, rode and boated his way from Calais through France and Italy to Venice and back via Switzerland, Germany and Holland, returning with that innovation the fork, which he had seen used in Italy. Coryate then wrote up his experiences in the waggishly titled *Coryat's Crudities* ('crudities' in the French sense meaning uncooked food), a book which proved to be nothing less than the first modern travel narrative. The *Crudities* and the European trip it was based on, were credited with starting the vogue for the Grand Tour, which later became an almost compulsory end to all good educations; a tradition of travel that has only become stronger and more widespread over the intervening years.

By way of an extended encore Coryate left England again in 1612, this time with India as his ultimate destination. The journey took him through the three most important Empires of the day: Ottoman, Persian and Mughal. He travelled first to Constantinople, where he spent almost a year, and from there on to the Holy Land by boat. He made a pilgrimage to Jerusalem before continuing east, this time bound for India. Eighteen months, and nearly 4,000 miles later, he was in the Mughal capital Agra, and almost unbelievably he had walked every step of the way.

But Coryate was not the most fortunate of men, despite his courage and his prescient travels. He didn't live to write the book of his Eastern journey, a book that would have surely made him a household name. His exertions and the privations of his mendicant lifestyle weakened him fatally, and in December 1617 he died in Surat, north of Bombay.

I had been interested in Thomas Coryate for some years since first stumbling across a reference to him in a West Country library. His biography, published in the Sixties and long out of print, reveals he was something of a character, immediately recognisable across the centuries as someone with an attractive, and attractively flawed, personality. He was both admired and ridiculed by his contemporaries, not least because he was from a humble background and rather puritanical by nature. But he was also an original, an archetype and a pioneer. It was that love of travel, and his single-minded pursuit of it, that drew me to him.

Since *Coryat's Crudities* countless thousands have repeated his European tour, not least a legion of 18th-century aristocrats. When I looked into it further it seemed that no one had yet recreated his journey to the East, and I became resolved to do this. I read and researched, scribbled notes in the British Library, collected references and excavated third-party texts. I found a copy of his last known writing, a sheaf of notes sent home from the Holy Land and five letters from India. I bought maps and pinned down the route he had taken and slowly my trip in his footsteps became a reality.

Somewhere along the line I made the decision that my trip should in some way live up to his legacy. Flying, or using any form of public transport, seemed almost an insult, yet I had no illusion that I could walk thousands of miles. The solution, once I had found it, was obvious and seemingly tailor-made. The trip was perfect for cycling. Doing the journey by bicycle would get me out in the elements, in among the people, involved in the world around me. I would live every curve of the road, defy the mountains, and endure the deserts. By cycling where Coryate walked, I would lay myself open to whatever came in a spirit that I felt was truly his.

So I followed Coryate to India, to Surat where he died five years into his last journey. I saw the countries he saw, the cities and the landscapes. I found some of the buildings he found, rode along many of the same roads and to some extent met the same people. Ancient empires merged with modern states as I rolled east on a journey Coryate and I now shared — a journey that began in Damascus.

Part 1

SYRIA, TURKEY AND THE OTTOMAN EMPIRE

During its heyday in the 16th century the Ottoman Empire included Turkey, the Levant and the Balkan Peninsula, as well as parts of the Caucasus, North Africa and Arabia.

Despite a reputation to the contrary in Europe, Ottoman society delighted in a refined and stylised civility. Comfort was a must-have to the *efendi*, 'professional man', who might have been seen relaxing on a divan with his feet up on an ottoman; or sipping coffee and puffing a water pipe in a coffee house, the first of which – effectively the first café – was opened in Istanbul in 1533.

The popular courtyard houses of the time allowed the separation of the *harem* – 'private quarters', where women could remain unveiled – from the public areas open to guests. The Turkish public bath house, or *hammam*, led eventually to European public baths and swimming pools, while the English dictionary took 'kismet' and 'turquoise', 'mammoth' and 'yoghurt' from Turkish.

Despite 'The Turk' being portrayed as a rabble in Europe, Ottoman society was highly structured. The Sultan headed society as an absolute ruler while below him a *vizier*, or administrative head, dealt with daily government and law, based on *sharia* (Islamic) principles. These controls gave enough order, and Ottoman conquest brought enough wealth, that many in the arts and the merchant classes were able to excel. It was during this period that men like the great architect Sinan (1489–1588) flourished, creating an aesthetic which today is considered quintessentially Ottoman.

The best-known of the Ottoman Sultans, Suleiman the Magnificent (r. 1520–66) was responsible for taking Turkey to the height of its military and cultural power. Later, in the 17th century, as Ottoman greatness began to wane, Europe began to retake territory she had previously lost. The Balkans were regained at this time, Persia recaptured western Iran and Russia annexed Azerbaijan. Slowly the political map began to change.

Today the Ottoman legacy lives on politically in the former Yugoslavia, where Islam came to Bosnia in the early 16th century.

1

Damascus: Roses and Refuse

The buttery flagstones of the mosque's courtyard had been polished to a dull sheen by centuries of passing feet. From the portico, where I sat shaded by a wide roof set on slender columns, the sun lit the stones and gleamed on the water of the ornamental pool. Even the flowers in the wide beds at the courtyard's edge seemed to shine, each leaf glinting separately in the Middle Eastern sun. Under the foliage yellow soil was baked to a crust and textured with brush marks where dead leaves were swept away each morning. Only the Damascus roses seemed to enjoy the heat, swaying gently with the breeze, their scent filling the air.

An empty echo of the city's cacophonous traffic drifted over the wall, quickly lost among the pleasanter sounds of the courtyard: the patter of the fountain, the murmur of conversation, the tinkling of glasses from the mosque's *shaihane* (teashop).

Like the damask and the eponymous roses the Tekkiye mosque is often overlooked by tourists in their rush to the Old City, although it is something of a favourite with locals. Just a couple of minarets and a stone wall from the outside, but inside every element was striking and memorable. Sinan, the 'Ottoman Christopher Wren' as he is often called, designed the building in the 1560s for the regional governor using a blend of familiar Ottoman elements and local features in a way that flattered both. The central dome and slender minarets, common in western Turkey, highlighted the courtyard, which was a purely Syrian detail; while the banded stonework and *muqarnas*, 'stalactite niches', above the main door, were more generally Muslim. Part of Sinan's ingenuity had been to position the pool in such a way as to encourage you to stand behind it, giving the building its proper perspective.

No doubt to Thomas Coryate – the grandfather, after all, of that cultural feast the Grand Tour – it would have been unmissable. I simply couldn't imagine him leaving Damascus without having seen the latest and greatest architectural marvel, especially when the architect was a household name (and therefore one he could have dropped to great effect at court).

Unfortunately, however, imagining Coryate in Damascus is exactly what I had to do because his own first-hand account, in the form of substantial notes made as he travelled, is largely absent.

He is known to have collected three sets of these notes during his Eastern trip. The first covered his time in the Holy Land including Damascus, and was the only one to see the light of day in any form; the second was sent home from Esfahan but lost before publication; the third was with Coryate at his death, though again these were lost.

That first collection, dealing with the Holy Land, found its way back to England and into print in a book called *Purchas His Pilgrims*, published in 1625. The book's author, Samuel Purchas, was a historian and occasional visitor to Prince Henry's court and the book a thorough and mildly jingoistic catalogue of English travel during the period. Here Coryate's account could sit alongside the great merchant travellers of the day, to be viewed – quite rightly – with equal respect. Except that true to Coryate's tragicomic lot in life, things went only partially according to this plan, largely because no one truly understood what he was doing. People were drawn abroad in those days only by the trinity of travel – commerce for the merchant, warfare for the soldier, pilgrimage for the pious. Coryate's personal endeavour came within no established field and, as a result, he came to be treated less as the high priest of independent travel and more like The Jester on tour. Consequently not all of his voluminous notes on the Holy Land were included in the *Pilgrims*. In fact Purchas cut the majority to ribbons.

There were already numerous accounts of the Holy Land by that time, albeit from pilgrims who immediately turned for home once the sights were seen, and consequently Purchas preferred not to include 'the rest of master Coryate's long, long journey [in the Holy Land] ... for fear you grow weary of him and me'. Purchas was more interested in wowing his readers with The Turk, a newly fashionable subject since the publication of *A General Historie of the Turkes* in 1603. This book was a large and detailed account of Ottoman history, pandering to the new English appetite for the empire of the cultured savage, and may in fact have influenced Coryate's own visit. Purchas duly prints Coryate's account of Constantinople, including much description of daily life and colour, but is less interested thereafter. Consequently Coryate has only just gone south from Aleppo on his pilgrimage when Purchas weighs in with the knife, intruding on a narrative already in full flow. 'His observations very very many I omit,' he says simply. By the time Coryate reaches Damascus he has left the seat of Ottoman dominance and is in a mere satellite state, and so without further ado Purchas abandons him.

The *Pilgrims* reads: '26th March – in Damascus I saw roses ...' But that is as far as Coryate gets with his description. We are robbed of the roses and indeed everything else because, as Purchas says, '... we have travelled with so many travellers to Damascus, and thence to Jeruselemm and observed so much on those parts, that I dare not obtrude Master Coryate's prolix-ity on the patientest reader.' Which is a shame because he then blithely confesses, 'I found much pleasure in walking with [Coryate] in his tenne dayes journey to Damascus, and in spending a little while to view his foure dayes view of Damascus.'

Sitting beside the slender columns of the portico, the lack of Coryate's own account allowed a certain freedom to daydream, and so I imagined that he too had come to the Tekkiye mosque. I found much pleas-ure of my own in the warm, perfumed air and the calming shade. And the mosque's beauty was made more poignant by a cruel twist to the story of the notes. It seems that in addition to the second and third sets going missing, the same fate eventually befell the first. At some point after Purchas had finished

13

with them, and possibly much later, they were overlooked as insignificant and mislaid, filed in a chest somewhere for mice and mildew to claim. Anyone searching for direct evidence of Coryate cannot but be disappointed here, especially as Purchas refers to the notes as '*bookes*' at one point, indicating that they might have been worked up to some degree. With the addition of five letters sent home from India and published around the time of his death, the Purchas material constitutes Coryate's entire legacy.

～

Thomas Coryate began his great and fateful journey in December 1612, sailing from England and arriving in Constantinople a full five months later. He spent ten months in the city as a guest of the English consul Sir Paul Pindar before sailing on to Scandroun, which is now Iskandrun in modern Turkey. From there he made his way inland to Aleppo and south, first to Damascus, and then to Jerusalem for an Easter pilgrimage in 1614. With the pilgrimage complete, Coryate returned to Damascus prior to going north.

I felt from the start that I should begin my journey in Damascus, and begin it in a way that somehow reflected the start of Coryate's. Given the time and effort it had taken him to reach Damascus, and my decision to travel in his spirit, it was obvious that I couldn't simply fly there. Other options such as sailing were not feasible given the timescale I had in mind. The solution was the train; a compromise that allowed me to arrive in the Middle East in a suitably battered fashion, although in five days rather than five months.

So I traded the Bay of Biscay and the Pillars of Hercules for Vienna's Westbahnhof and Istanbul's Haydarpaşa stations, clattering across Europe to arrive in Damascus in the muggy darkness of a summer evening. Without a decent map or any directions (or bicycle lights) I made my way through the mayhem that is Damascene traffic to Suq Sarouja, formerly a market and one of the oldest parts of the city, now home to the cheaper hotels.

After that spectral night-time spin the Tekkiye mosque was the perfect place to relax and regain my land legs. Its self-contained calm and modest proportions emphasised the building's humanity, adding to the restful atmosphere. The mosque itself was venerable now and remained closed for all but Friday prayers, though while I was enjoying the shade a mullah arrived to give the midday *adhan*, the call to prayer, using a microphone that was locked in a box beside the door. A dozen or so men made their ablutions and came into the portico to pray, and because there was not the slightest hint that I should leave at this point, I stayed, feeling a little humbled by the courtesy.

And now that I looked out into the courtyard again, that too seemed less formal. Office workers in western dress bustled through on their way to lunch, families mooched around and a young couple held hands. A schoolteacher wearing a *chador* – the all-over covering that is compulsory in Iran – marshalled a group of children across the flags and sat them along the pool's low wall. She then held forth on (presumably) the beauty and significance of the building while the children splashed each other and generally paid less than full attention.

Despite the mosque's architecture and the impression given by people dressed like the school teacher, Syria is officially not an Islamic but a secular state. The ruling Ba'ath 'renaissance' party has run the country as a socialist dictatorship for thirty years, and while it is true that virtually all Ba'athists are Muslims, religion is not the party's primary identity.

Between Independence in 1946 and the end of the Sixties Syria had stumbled from government to government, into and out of the ill-conceived 'United Arab Republic' with Egypt, through a period of Soviet friendship and on to the bloodless coup in 1970 that installed Hafez Assad. After his death in 2000 the dictatorship passed peacefully to his unassuming heir Bashar, who has held it ever since.

The Assad dictatorship is unusual in the Middle East because it has lasted so long, and because it is that of a minority group – and a minority by a long way. The Assad family is part of Syria's Alawite community, an Islamic sect little known elsewhere and making up just 10 per cent of the population. (Christians account for another 10 per cent and Sunni Muslims the balance.) The Alawites follow a secretive canon which includes belief that the twelfth Imam – the *Mahdi* – a lost descendant of Ali, will return one day to reveal the Truth. This belief relates to the Shia veneration of Ali, the cousin and son-in-law of Muhammad, with the important addition that Ali is an incarnation of God rather than a prophet. Centuries ago the Alawites retreated into the hills near Aleppo with their beliefs, keeping themselves apart until the French, who appreciated their westernised sensibilities, promoted them prior to the Second World War. By the time of independence the Alawites were part of most institutions and government offices; from there it was only a matter of time, and the ruthlessness of Hafez Assad, before they came to power.

As the son of a priest, Coryate more than most would have appreciated the religious nature of this. Religion in early 17th century England was intrinsically woven into every aspect of life in a way that is hard to appreciate today. Yet I was to see this interdependence in the Islamic countries of Coryate's journey, where the inseparability of Church and State, or at least the attempt to forge it, is the bedrock of society. It was in places like the Tekkiye mosque, where religion and a universal aesthetic come together so well, that I got my first glimpse of what this meant in practical terms.

⌒

After that blissful afternoon in the mosque I spent a couple of days sightseeing, looking for the city I had read about in books such as T E Lawrence's *The Seven Pillars of Wisdom*.

'Damascus,' he wrote, 'had the name of an earthly paradise to the tribes who could enter it only after weeks and weeks of painful marching ...' I pictured the heroes of the Arab revolt braving the deserts and I wanted Damascus to be like that: Bedouin tents, bellowing camels, crystal streams.

It was said that the *Ghouta*, the fragrant and fertile plain surrounding the old city, was so lovely that

Muhammad himself turned aside lest he be tempted from his path to Paradise by this earthly wonder. Benjamin Tudelensis, one of many visiting medieval pilgrims mentioned two streams, one of which, the 'Pharphar [Barada River], running by the city itself, doth water all the gardens and pleasant places'. Coryate too came across two streams flowing, as he put it, 'to the houses, whereof above one thousand conduits of most pure water are thence conveyed'. But the only water I found was snaking through refuse below the north wall of the Old City, and the only fragrance that of petrol. Since the Ottoman redevelopment of the city, the Barada's public life has all but finished. The river is now relegated to gutters below the concrete city centre and suffers badly from drought in summer (and all year from Damascenes heaving their garbage into it). I had to admit it was a shock. What had once been a fabled city in an oasis of angelic greenery was now a sprawling urban accretion.

This, or something similar, was on Ammar's mind when I met him in the mid-afternoon crescendo of heat. I came out of an alley in Suq Sarouja just as he raised a mobile phone to his ear and we collided. Ammar was mortified to have bumped into a 'guest' in Syria and insisted he bought tea as an apology. We

19

went to a *shaihane* on a nearby rooftop and looked out over the haze.

'Damascus is more like a building site than a pilgrimage site,' he said, nodding at a concrete monstrosity across the road. 'That building has been unfinished for five years. It is a government building.'

Concrete floors showed through tattered tarpaulins like the ribs of a carcass.

'And the houses here?' I asked, meaning Suq Sarouja.

'It costs too much money for people to restore old houses, so they pull them down and build new ones, but they don't renovate. In the Old City it is different. People have more money and there is some foreign investment. The city and the government help with money there too, but not in Suq Sarouja.'

Ammar was an even-tempered man with a bloodhound face and a repertoire of melancholy expressions. He ran an interior design company and knew the city from the inside out.

'Things are always being built in Damascus,' he said.

'Except that place,' I replied, nodding at the government building. 'That's stuck half way.'

He raised his glass to his lips and looked over the rim. 'It will be mostly for Shia pilgrims from Iran, I think.'

Though I had not been in Syria long I felt this was a hint.

'So you think it may never be finished? Or perhaps used for something else? The government's relations with Iran – are they good?'

They were good. Good enough for Syria and Iran to have a relationship that has a particular place on the world stage; for Iran to act as financier to some of Syria's dirtier tricks in third-party countries like Lebanon, and for the relationship to be a worry to many countries inside and outside the region. They had also been good enough for Iran to send troops from its elite Revolutionary Guard to establish and train Hezbollah, the quintessential Middle Eastern terror-ist group, and for those troops to help eject Israeli forces from southern Lebanon. Some of the same men then went on to softer targets and were involved in the kidnapping of John McCarthy, Brian Keenan and Terry Waite among others. But despite this special relationship the Syrian government still exhibits a certain amount of paranoia, that hallmark of a good dictatorship. The thought of busloads of Shia arriving each day to stay in the heart of the capital was a little unnerving, even if they were pilgrims.

Ammar did not say this. No Syrian would presume to second-guess his government's private business, which is what foreign affairs are in Syria. What he said was, 'Maybe the government will change its mind. You know how governments are. The pilgrims come for the Umayyad mosque in the Old City because it is the holiest shrine to them after Mecca. Did you know John the Baptist's head is there? And there are other sights in Old Damascus too. That is the real Damascus, you know, the Old City: the Damascus of the Bible. And this,' he waved a hand to indicate Suq Sarouja, 'was the first part built outside the old walls.'

The modern city has grown up around them both, although too much of it had grown up recently, in a period when common sense and any desire for planned expansion had apparently deserted everyone in favour of 'development and progress', as Syria's only English-language newspaper called it.

Like most Damascenes Ammar lived in one of these Development and Progress apartment blocks in the suburbs. He came into the city for his English lessons and to chat with foreign tourists. If these tourists were English, he made a special place for them in his schedule. He was in Suq Sarouja to quote for renovation work and had been calling his client when we met. He would have preferred work in the Old City, he said, but it was difficult to break into that market.

The Department of Antiquities bought properties there and paid for them to be renovated. It was the government's obligation to Syrian history to ensure that this unique area, the oldest part of the world's oldest city, didn't fall into ruin. The work was well paid because of this government interest, but you had to be established to get it, you had to have a name and know the right people.

Ammar gave me another of his sad faces. His business was small and new, and he couldn't compete with the larger and more established firms. He made the point that despite this, all his customers were happy, and produced a sheaf of photographs showing neat interiors. Low ceilings, beams, white plasterwork, all slightly reminiscent of English Tudor. He couldn't break into the Old City so he hoped to make a name for himself in Suq Sarouja. He felt it would be the next area to go big.

It certainly had the potential. The architecture was similar to the Old City and in places almost as old. Most of the original houses were Ottoman, the best of which were in the courtyard style and constructed of familiar black and white banded stone, solid and simple with some evocative detail. Cheaper versions of brick and plaster were now decidedly tired, and all were crammed together into fractured alleyways and streets that held the city like a net. In the Damascene heat wattle and daub crumbled, gable ends bowed, door frames dropped and windows gaped. There was a lifetime's work here for someone in the building trade.

◞

After our first meeting Ammar appointed himself my fixer in Damascus. He made sure I knew where the museums were, translated for me, recommended a book and even scanned newspapers in case there was an English film showing. And when I mentioned that I needed an Iranian visa he looked up the address of the embassy and organised a lift.

'*Safar Irani* is out of the centre on the Beirut road, a very big road. You must not cycle there, Danny, the traffic will be very dangerous.'

He thought for a moment.

'A friend of mine could take you. Yes, I'm sure he will.' Then, with a smile smoothing out his jowls like a face-lift: 'You will go in style.'

Style turned out to be a hugely swerving Chevrolet driven by a compact and business-like Kurd. The car was at least 40 years old, had four bald tyres and was the size of a small bus. I watched nervously as it veered across the road towards me, the driver, Tariq, already calling out as the car wallowed to a halt.

'Get in,' he said, 'Get in. I am Ammar's friend. I will take you to the embassy.'

As we hurtled getaway-style from the kerb I made a reflexive swipe for a seatbelt, only to find there weren't any, then tried to brace my legs in the vast footwell. I was reduced to eyeing the dashboard nervously with my fingers clamped to the blood-red vinyl of the seat.

Tariq was a taxi driver by trade, on a day off. Ammar had persuaded him to take me because he could persuade another friend to lend Tariq the car. So we drove through the streets of Damascus in the Syrian equivalent of a stretch limo, Tariq's square jaw and stubble giving him the look of a cartoon gangster, my pasty face framed in the windscreen like a kidnap victim.

We drove west, away from Suq Sarouja and the nearby Old City I'd come to know, out through city centre shops, airline offices and government buildings.

After an initial burst of enthusiasm, in which he questioned me about English football, Tariq fell into a ruminative silence. To encourage him, and in an attempt to calm his driving, I asked about his family. Did he have brothers or sisters? He nodded curtly and gave a snort – don't talk to me about sisters. His exasperation was not at his sister but on her behalf. She was studying English at university and she was having some problems. Not of her own making, I should understand, problems 'from the government'. Tariq was fond of his sister and told me that she was a good student, two years into a degree and at the top of her class. She had taught Tariq some English and he was proud of her for that, and grateful (Ammar now taught Tariq his English). Her problem was that she was without job prospects, or at least prospects of a graduate's job. Anyone could work in a *shwarma* (kebab) shop or drive a taxi, Tariq said, but someone with a university education should have a proper job.

'We have no rights, some of us' he said. 'Many people migrated after the war and changed where they lived. They moved between Turkey, Syria and other places and my father came into Syria then. He came when he was a boy with my grandfather, but they never applied for a passport so later my father was made an *ajnabi*, a "foreigner". But he had lived in Syria all his life! Now all my family are "foreign". We cannot vote, we cannot buy land and we cannot get government jobs.'

Kurds like Tariq sometimes led a marginal existence in the Middle East, where they live in an area centred in northern Iraq but which spills over into

Iran, Turkey and Syria. They are a people with a strong identity, a long history and an ancient, now Muslim, culture. With 25 million in the region they are the largest ethnic group anywhere without a state. All of which caused a certain amount of nervousness in the four governments under which they live.

'Do you know some of us can't even use hospitals or schools?' Tariq said. 'They have no ID cards at all, so they don't exist. They are called *maktoumeen*. It means "hidden" in Arabic but in Syria the meaning is "unregistered". The government doesn't admit they exist.'

Tariq talked about various friends who were unemployed, had bad jobs or were otherwise disadvantaged, and his complaints became a litany of disgust. Having a grievance made him willing to blame the government for everything. He compared what Hafez Assad, the old dictator, had done to Kurdish aspirations with what Saddam Hussein had done to the Iraqi Kurds. I thought this was a bit much and pointed out that the Syrian government had so far gassed no one, neither did it seem about to.

Tariq turned to me as we thundered along the hot tarmac, his hands squeezing the wheel as though he were wringing someone's neck.

'But Qamishli ...' he said simply.

27

Nothing like as many Kurds had died in Qamishli, in Syria's remote north-eastern quarter, as in Iraq, but they had died none the less. In March 2004 with Iraq under nominal allied control, Kurds in neighbouring countries began to see a chink of daylight. A democratic Iraq could bring the rights that Kurds everywhere aspired to. A potential problem for other governments in the region, to the extent that discontent began to rumble underground in the north-east, Syria's main Kurdish area.

What changed Qamishli from a place name into an event had started with a football match. Kurds are fanatical about football and the game in question was a local derby, a grudge match between an Arab and a Kurdish team. A riot broke out after the match and first the stadium, then the town, were engulfed. There were rumours that elements of Syrian *Mukhabarrat*, the 'specialist police', had previously armed some of the town's Arabs and that a hard core of Kurds had done the same for themselves. Whatever the truth of these claims the situation quickly became a bloodbath in which dozens died on both sides, though official accounts drastically downplayed the numbers.

Nor was this the first time the Syrian Kurds felt aggrieved. For some time they had suffered various indignities as the government changed Kurdish place names to Arabic names, encouraged Arab settlers to move into Kurdish areas and even set up wholly new Arab villages. To add insult to injury, these new settlements often received exactly the kind of investment that Kurdish villages lacked.

Tariq calmed down a little when I sympathised with him and concentrated on his driving for a while.

Away from the centre the Al-Mazzah highway was lined with blank-faced housing blocks that were half turned from the road as if lacking the courage to face the traffic. The angle made them seem interesting, as though walking between them would lead to somewhere worth going.

Above them on a barren hillside a low-rise fortress of a building glowered over the city.

'It's called *People's Palace*,' said Tariq venomously, 'but only one person lives there.' The palace was an ugly building even by the high standards of Damascus and had the air of a concrete bunker put to other use. Though apparently to mitigate the threat of Israeli assassination the President moved, *Führer*-style, between this and other locations at random.

'That is the Iranian embassy,' said Tariq suddenly, waving a hand at a building across the road. We drifted across all three lanes to the tune of much plaintive honking and came to a halt at a set of traffic lights. Tariq made a U-turn, scattering more traffic, and pulled up outside the embassy. He would come back in an hour, he said as I left the car. I mentioned half an hour but Tariq was resolute: things always took longer then they should at the Iranian embassy.

When I came out an hour later he was waiting patiently, the car's radio blaring.

'You didn't get the visa?' he said, as I walloped the door shut. A screech of tyres somewhere behind us signified that we had left the kerb.

'They've asked me to go back in a couple of days. I think they'll give it to me then,' I said. Tariq was fooled neither by my bluster nor the embassy's vague request, and he was spot on. I went back three days later by bicycle – Tariq was busy driving his taxi and the Chevrolet had broken down – only to be told that the visa was not ready. My enquiry was brushed aside in favour of a lecture on the uphill battle Iranians faced when applying for British visas.

Suitably chastened, but privately fuming, I rode back to Suq Sarouja. Despite my best intentions, not to mention all the planning and preparation I'd done at home, it seemed I might already be coming unstuck. To add to my bureaucratic woes my Syrian visa was expiring, and although the country is comparatively small it was still a week's cycling to the Turkish border.

It didn't help my state of mind to know that this border is a modern invention and that Coryate would not have known of it. He would simply have walked from the Tekkiye mosque back to his caravan, which was camped in the *Ghouta* below the city wall, and walked with it into Turkey, then just another part of the Ottoman Empire. Neither would he have needed a visa, then or at any point on his journey. Visas were unknown, as in fact were passports, the modern versions of which came into being only with the First World War. In the 17th century a passport – literally permission to pass through the ports to go abroad – was a single document issued directly by the Crown for a specific journey. Today, partly because of Coryate's adventures, travel is an integral part of modern life.

So feeling that hanging about for visas was just not Coryatesque enough, and piqued by a second embassy request to come back 'in a few days', I gave in to my desire to begin the journey. The visa could wait: it would sort itself out. That evening I paid my hotel bill, filled all six water bottles to the brim and set my alarm. By 4.30 the next morning I was cycling in the desert.

2

Hama Horror

The experience was worth waiting for. This was the desert Lawrence had talked about, the desert that killed camels and drove men mad. The desert that protected Damascus to the south, covered the whole of the Syrian interior and went east in one form or another almost as far as India. A mustard-coloured desolation of shallow hills and broken rock that went all the way to the trembling horizon. Only a line of black tarmac betrayed Man's presence, and the gleaming cars that crawled back and forth were a comfort.

By nine o'clock the desert was limitless in the sun, and daunting after the close and soon familiar chaos of Damascus. On the plateau away from the city the road dragged across a series of long and deadly slopes. Each rise gave way to the next imperceptibly with nothing truly flat in between and never a gradient steep enough to coast down. Despite the particular form of fatigue the hot dry winds induced, I found myself reluctant to stop. It was such a singular environment, this harsh arid steppe, and everything in it so new, that fascination easily drew me on.

There were four days of this landscape between Damascus and Aleppo, in some places like an abandoned quarry, in others like a beach at low tide. To be fair there were also two major cities and numerous villages, though riding through them really only emphasised how much the desert qualified everything. The streets of Homs, the first city after Damascus, were desert streets even though the city was a characterless mass of concrete and the steppe a kilometre away.

Hama, 40 kilometres further north, had the character that Homs lacked, helped in no small measure by the Orontes River. Hama had grown up over thousands of years on its banks and somehow felt more in tune with the desert around it. In town, aqueducts dating from the Roman period teetered on heavy stone pillars and *norias* – giant waterwheels like fairground Ferris wheels – creaked and groaned as they lifted water up to the channels.

That playful sloshing could have been Hama's motif, were it not for the dark secret hidden in the accompanying groan from the *norias'* wooden axles. A secret that also explained some of the things I'd noticed around town, like why there were no longer *madrassas* (religious schools) there and why the old quarter was so small.

In 1982 Hama had been the victim of a three-day bombing campaign that levelled parts of the city and killed as many as 30,000 people. Conflict is unfortunately a theme in the Middle East but these bombs were not part of an invasion, they came from Syrian artillery and from Syrian fighter jets.

Hafez Assad, the 'Old Lion' as people liked to think of him, had instructed his brother Rifaat to clear Hama of the Muslim Brotherhood, a terrorist group holed up in the old city. But the army was attacked when it entered the narrow streets in an ambush that killed dozens of soldiers. Rifaat reacted like a true psychotic. He unleashed everything he had, bringing the old city down on the heads of the people in it, the great majority of whom were nothing to do with terrorism, or even the Muslim Brotherhood: they just happened to live there. The population of Hama was 200,000 at the time: 15 per cent of a decent-sized city was wiped out in three days by its own government.

I heard this story from Munif in a busy *shaihane* in Aleppo a couple of days from Hama. I was recovering from the desert, drinking constantly and staying in the shade and Munif was on the lookout for foreigners.

He was a PhD student in his late twenties and a guide to the local ruins.

It was not the kind of story you heard in Hama, Munif said. No one talked about it because it was impossible to do so without criticising the old President, and Syrians just didn't do that.

'In Syria we have what we call the red lines,' he said. 'It means there are some things you just can't do – you can't cross a red line. One of these lines is that you can't question the President. He is like a God or something. It is because of the traditional Arabic attitude of respect for leaders and the old attitudes to power, which still apply today. And you certainly can't try to kill the President, which is what the Brotherhood did. When they tried to do that, they had to be taught a lesson.

'Do you know the Assads are from Latakia, on the coast? There has always been rivalry between Latakia and Hama. At the coast people are more relaxed, less religious. They think Hama people are stuck-up snobs.' Munif giggled. 'In Hama,' he said, reversing his upturned palm, 'they say Latakia people are the stupid cousins, that they are tasteless and tactless. Maybe this also had something to do with what happened. Perhaps some very old scores were settled, who knows.'

I asked Munif if he felt any sympathy either way.

'I am from Aleppo,' he beamed, 'it is the European city of Syria, and the academic city. This is the place I prefer – but you are the visitor, which place do you prefer?'

My four days from Damascus had brought my first camping experience, a breathlessly hot dust-bowl a little way from the road protected on the windward side by a *tell*, a mound (often a burial mound) that was just one of the many hundreds that pepper the Syrian landscape with forgotten history. Seemingly as a reward I had spent the next night in a five-star hotel in the middle of nowhere, a miraculous coincidence not only because of the swimming pool, cavernous air-conditioned room and 100-channel TV, but also because the manager refused to let me pay. 'You will stay here tonight,' he had said, slapping me on my sweaty shoulder, 'not as my guest, but as a guest of the Syrian people.'

I relayed this to Munif, and told him about Ammar's help in Damascus. So far all of Syria seemed pretty good to me.

He smiled again, his round face like a baby's.

'Hospitality is formal respect,' he said. 'It's the other side of the coin from what happened in Hama. It makes Syrian people welcoming but also makes us too quiet. You know we have no idea about democracy;

but also we don't want to know. This country is good without it.'

It was disappointing to hear, but he had a point. Syria was one of the safest and friendliest countries I'd ever been in. You could almost knock on a door at random and ask to come in, so warm was the welcome given to foreigners.

∽

When I arrived in Aleppo the temperature went up to 40°C and stayed there. I shuffled around the city's distinctly French streets with my head bowed, waiting for the weight to be lifted. But relief never came and in its place I came down with heat stroke. The result was four days in bed feeling sorry for myself, with the air-conditioning full on and a wet towel over my head. Although the time did at least allow me to go through some of the background notes I had with me.

Purchas His Pilgrims made it clear that Coryate didn't linger in Aleppo on his first visit, though once he returned in May 1614, after the pilgrimage, he spent four months here.

During his stay it is also likely that Coryate was coming to a decision about what he would do next. It would be tempting to say that he left England bound for India, but it would also probably be inaccurate.

He specifically says he is heading for Constantinople and the Holy Land when he leaves, but makes no mention of any further destination.

Unfortunately Coryate's thoughts, and indeed all of his four months in Aleppo, must remain conjecture. Purchas has had what he wants in the descriptions of Constantinople and there is little space left for the oddball from Odcombe. Purchas sums up and moves on. 'His journey from thence [Jerusalem, after the pilgrimage] to Aleppo and thence into Mesopotamia, Persia, India, you have before related in his own epistles.'

And that's it. Done. From here on Coryate appears in history only through those epistles (his five letters from India), and through the occasional musings of those he met while toiling inexorably eastward.

With nothing further from Purchas, looking for Coryate in Aleppo was like looking for water in the desert. Once I was over the heat stroke and no longer felt like a hypochondriac in a Victorian novel, I ventured out to the national museum in the centre of town. Although they were helpful, all they could find relating to Coryate was my own letter, written from the UK months earlier and scrupulously cross-referenced. And I failed at the Gregorian Armenian church too, in the Armenian *suq*, because its ageing

39

square door, banded and studded with black iron and set into gorgeous butter-coloured stonework, was resolutely locked. Munif had recommended the church because he said it kept historical records back to the 17th century, although of course to see such records you first had to get inside. I stood at the door looking helpless in the hope that another Ammar would pass by, but no one came. After a couple of minutes I gave up and went into a nearby silversmith's to ask for help. The smith looked up as I went in, a loupe in one eye, engraving pick in one hand, silver eggcup in the other. The church was closed, he said, and went back to his work. I asked if it was ever open but he just said 'closed'.

I walked south into the chaotic streets heading away from Jdeide, the Christian quarter, towards the main *suq*. I had not gone far when a rotund man with an alabaster face and a black moustache fell in step beside me. He waited until I noticed him and spoke in English.

'I know your Brighton,' he said when I told him where I was from, 'I studied economics there. A one-year postgraduate course.' He spoke in a clipped precise way that was a mish-mash of East and West so that Brighton rhymed with 'right on'.

'I studied abroad because it is the thing to do.

Study and improve your skills, it gives you better chances. And it is an Armenian thing to do. We have always tried to get on and in Syria there are opportunities. We are bankers, d'you know, and we have many other businesses in the city – you can see from the Armenian script on the signs. I have a shop in the Armenian *suq*.' He waved a hand back the way we'd come. 'We have a little security here now because Aleppo is still the main trading city in Syria. And because there is no persecution, not like it was in Turkey.'

The man bobbed his head in confirmation. The moustache, together with his accent and deferential manner, gave him a comic resemblance to Hercule Poirot.

Because he had mentioned Turkey I asked if his family had been affected during the last days of the Ottoman Empire.

'Everyone was involved.' He said emphatically. 'Everyone. My grandfather was lucky to survive that period. He and my great grandmother came from Turkey, d'you know. This was many years ago of course after the First World War. Ever since then my family has been in the Armenian *suq*.'

I thought he was hinting that we go back to his shop so I pressed on in the opposite direction.

'You must be going to see the big *suq*,' the man said in his matter-of-fact way. Every visitor to Aleppo ended up there eventually; it was why Coryate called the city 'the principal emporium of all Syria, or rather the orient world'.

The man, whose name was Karekin, kept pace beside me on short triangular legs, talking enthusiastically as we went. His family had lived for generations near Bitlis, a small prosperous town near Lake Van, in far-eastern Turkey, as shopkeepers and traders. Then during the First World War his family was dragged into the mire of international politics. As the Ottoman Empire went through its death throes, Turks, especially those in the army, abandoned caution. Spurred on by the actions of a few Armenian revolutionaries, themselves often acting as proxies for Russia, Turkey began a full-scale pogrom. In August 1915 the *New York Times* reported a massacre of as many as 40,000 men, women and children in the Bitlis area. Many were marched to a nearby tributary of the Tigris and shot into the river. Others were driven out of their homes and told not to return. The only hope of survival for many thousands was escape to the south, out of the *Vilayet* (province) of Van and into the more moderate *Vilayet* of Aleppo.

'This is the Bab Antakya, the Antioch gate,'

Karekin said looking up at a tiny two-storey castle. 'Through here is Suq al-Attarin, it was the *decumanus* [the main east-west street] in Roman times – that's how old Aleppo is.'

The gate had a wonderfully simple design that defied attackers with a dog-leg passage through to the street beyond. Crenellations, loopholes and a huge wooden gate peppered with iron studs completed the pocket fortress look. Through the gateway the market stretched away east for a mile to the ancient citadel with tributaries off the main street totalling something like five miles in length.

The blaring music and screaming traffic of the street died away inside, replaced by the gentler sounds of barter and business. The *suq* took on a subterranean feel just a few yards from the gate, with shops and stalls shoehorned into tiny recesses in the ancient brickwork. A shop selling spices might be crammed beside one selling dried fruit or rice, or cooking oils, or copper goods, vegetables, fish, clothing; it didn't matter what the shop sold, they all fought for space on the cobbles. Where we entered, the bags, rope and tent cloth of one stall were winning their battle against a barrow, while the owner of another held his stall steady as a donkey with pencil thin legs pushed past. A little further on a butcher had nailed a goat's entrails to a door above a neat row of sheep heads.

'This was originally smaller,' Karekin called back as he squeezed past a precarious stack of televisions. 'The *suq* was expanded in the 13th century by Ghazni, Saladin's son [Saladin who defeated the Crusaders]. He fortified the city and made it what it is today.'

I stepped around a pile of potatoes and stopped for a moment beside a crooked passageway leading down to an 11th-century *madrassa*. From the vaulted ceiling above, broad columns of sunlight struck downwards looking in the gloom like a gorgeous liquid. Dingy and crammed, this was unmistakably the bazaar of legend, the bazaar that had tantalised travellers east of Vienna for so many centuries, and even enticed some of them to pass this way. It couldn't have looked very different when Coryate came here, which he surely did. I could only imagine what his descriptions would have told us about Syrian life of the period. In consolation I stood for a while enjoying this truly unique place, one in which I was as close to the 17th century as it was possible to be.

Every commodity under the sun had come through these caverns at one time or another; everything that man had ever desired or traded in or could make a profit from. And beneath those brick vaults even the most mundane items gained a kind of nobility. For a while our conversation stopped as I took in my surroundings, intoxicated by the feeling of participating in history.

'It was Ghazni who dug the great moat around the citadel,' Karekin explained when we moved on. 'Then he built up a massive rampart and made the citadel impregnable.' Ghazni had been a shrewd man and he prepared Aleppo for the worst. At the same time he had sought to insulate the city from possible problems by forging trading relationships in the region. He contracted Venetian merchants to move goods from Aleppo to the coast and then sail them to Europe. He ensured that business came through Aleppo in one way or another so that when commercial shipping caused the decline of the Silk Road, the city remained an important trading post.

My attention was caught by a stall selling the most exquisite cutlery imaginable, or so it seemed to my goggling eyes. I wondered if I could justify buying an engraved fish slice and a baking tray ... surely nothing from the Aleppo *suq* could ever be useless.

We threaded our way through the mêlée with Karekin pointing out details here and there. He seemed intent on small talk now and when he didn't return to the story of his family I asked him directly.

He touched his moustache and looked at me as though no one had asked this before.

'My grandfather was fourteen when those massacres took place, d'you see. That's how he escaped. Any man over fourteen was taken by the Turks and killed. Systematically', he parried a finger in the air, 'because that's what they deny now, that it was systematic. They say it was random fighting, that only 200,000 Armenians died, that Armenians killed as many Turks.' He gave an indignant snort. 'Two hundred thousand ...'

He lapsed into a morose silence that was accentuated by the noise around us. The massacres he was referring to had taken place between 1915 and 1922 as the Ottoman Empire crumbled. They were an attempt, by the fragmenting Empire, to rid itself of its undesirable elements and emerge from the wreckage of war as a single nation. The result is often called the 20th century's first genocide.

To lighten the mood I asked Karekin if he knew anything about Bitlis as it currently was as I would be there in a few weeks.

'Ah', he said more brightly, 'you are a backpacking traveller, wandering about the country like Marco Polo or someone.'

I jumped at the chance and explained that I was

following another great traveller, an Englishman who had come through the area and continued all the way to India on foot. I explained that Coryate had been called the first backpacker and that he was very well known in his day. I asked if Karekin had heard of Thomas Coryate.

He touched his moustache again and said 'Hmm' in an almost studied parody of Poirot. I half expected him to say, 'I have deduced that the killer is ...', but all he said was a disappointing 'no'.

As we walked on through the *suq* Karekin returned to the story of his family.

'Some of the men from my grandfather's village escaped the first killings because they worked in other places as labourers. When they heard what was happening of course they went home, only to be killed themselves in many cases. My grandfather was ill as a child and so he was small – this was what saved him. The Turks thought he was young so they let him go. At that time my family lived south of Bitlis and this also helped because the Turks came from the west, from Adana, and billeted in Bitlis town. My family and other people in their village had a little time to escape so they left their homes and went wherever they could. That suited the Turks because it made Armenian property easier to take.

'They walked, my grandfather and his mother, 400 miles from Bitlis to Aleppo. My grandfather had no shoes and after the first week neither did my great-grandmother. Then my grandfather was ill and had to be carried. I said he was small but my great-grandmother carried him for days, then she was too tired and someone else in the group carried him. Sometimes they could ride in a cart but still it took them a month to come to Aleppo. When they got here it was autumn and very cold and my grandfather had pneumonia. He was never healthy.

'When my grandfather was twenty-one my great-grandmother gave him some money, and when she died he opened a shop selling Armenian artefacts. This is the shop that I have now.'

I asked about the Armenians still living in Turkey but Karekin said there were very few. Perhaps 30,000 people out of a total population of 70 million. Armenians were leaving all the time, often for America or to come to Aleppo. If they didn't take their possessions with them they gave them to friends and the rest came to Karekin to sell. Nothing was left behind in Turkey.

'You know in one way we have cut ourselves off from our past.' Karekin continued. 'We don't think Turkey is our home any more and we don't miss it. Now we have Armenia, if we want to go there, although they have their problems too. And we have our memories.' Then, acknowledging the fascination of the *suq*. 'This is our history now – we have adopted it. We have been here for three or four generations already and we will stay. We are happy with Assad.' He saw my expression and laughed.

⁋

Thomas Coryate was born into respectable, if unre-markable, country stock. His father, George, studied at Oxford where he distinguished himself as a lan-guage scholar. But if there was an opportunity to capitalise on his success, George did not take it. He seems to have preferred a life of pastoral dedication, and he remained the village priest in Odcombe until slipping selflessly from history in 1607.

From this humble background the rather more ambitious Thomas, born from his father's second marriage, made his way first to Winchester College and on to Oxford University's Gloucester Hall, now Worcester College. There are no records of Coryate's time here, although it was noted elsewhere that he had a head for the classics, a prodigious memory and an affinity for languages. Despite these credentials Coryate went down without taking a degree, and although this was more common at the time it must have still disappointed his father. Not only because university educations were self-funded, and expensive, but also because a degree was a prerequisite for joining the clergy. It seems that the younger Coryate had already set himself on an altogether different path.

After coming down from Oxford in the last years of the 1500s or the first years of the new century, Coryate returned to Odcombe and apparently settled into country life. There is little information about exactly what he did at this time, but his father's income as a country parson would not have supported him for long, and so it seems he took gainful employment somewhere. In all likelihood this was local and perhaps took the form of teaching in one of the nearby villages, if not in Odcombe itself.

During this period Coryate became better acquainted with the local gentry, including the Phelips family at Montacute House a short walk from Odcombe's vicarage. Both father and son, Edward and Robert, had been made knights by King James I in 1603 and had continued to rise in the world since then. Edward's parliamentary career flourished and he became Master of the Rolls, while Robert took up a position as a body servant to Henry, Prince of Wales.

Coryate's introduction to the young Prince Henry's court almost certainly came from this friendship, probably with Robert, closer to Coryate's own age and already a member of Henry's household. Prince Henry was well known at the time as a precocious talent, who by the age of nine had his own court staffed by dozens of servants. He was an avowed Protestant with a thirst for knowledge who excelled in the martial sports and scholarship alike. Perhaps most importantly Henry was not opposed to the kind of learning that was then coming from travel. His court was known as a place where the famous merchants of the day told their tales, no doubt to Coryate's increasing delight.

What direct information there is about Coryate from this period at court comes largely from posthumous sources and often does not bear scrutiny. The authors were all writing after Coryate's death and tended to repeat hand-me-down information without much care for corroboration. All too often they relied solely on hearsay.

One of the few physical descriptions of Coryate comes from such a source, a Bishop Thomas Fuller, who included Coryate in his *History of the Worthies of England*. Coryate was laughably ugly, Fuller tells us, with a head, 'like a sugar-loaf inverted, with the little end before'. The only problem with this description is that the two men never met. In fact Fuller was just three when Coryate left England in 1612. Still later authors compounded the same mistakes until Coryate was altered beyond all recognition. He was a dwarf, some said, and he visited places as far afield as Iraq, Africa and Central Asia, all of which are inaccurate, although they do illustrate how the myth of Coryate grew and has ultimately outlived him.

In the case of looks the obvious arbiter is a portrait by the London engraver William Hole, now held in the National Portrait Gallery in London. The likeness was used as the centrepiece for the title plate of *Coryat's Crudities* and is detailed enough to be considered accurate. The picture shows a healthy looking man in his early thirties dressed in fashionable clothes. Perhaps he is a little narrow-jawed, with a forehead made for learning, but he certainly does not resemble a sugar loaf.

Coryate continued at court for several years, 'serving in his own clothes' (Fuller again) which basically meant at his own expense. There is no clue as to what he did for money in London, expensive then as now, so it seems he either had a sponsor or earned a living in some way, again perhaps by teaching. Fuller says that Prince Henry 'allowed him a pension and kept him for a servant', though this may not be accurate either as court records show only one payment of £10 being made to Coryate. Although £10 equates to approximately £3,000 today, it would not have gone far, especially as he could have been at court for as much as five years.

～

It took another day for me to finally succumb to Munif's overtures and join him on one of his tours, as I had known I would from the start. The centre piece of the trip, and the reason I was going, was the mosaic museum in Ma'arat, an hour from Aleppo. It was a chance to see for myself some of the best-preserved early Christian symbols, a fascinating subject for anyone interested in the history of travel. Combined with other evidence from language, these crosses chart a significant episode in human history.

The key to unlocking this part of our travelling past was something discovered in 1786 by Sir William Jones, a British civil servant in India. Jones had noticed similarities between Sanskrit, of which he was a scholar, and Latin and Greek, in which he was proficient (along with thirty-odd other languages). He proposed that these similarities were more than just coincidence, and that in fact they showed a relationship between the languages. Jones further proposed that all three languages were descended from a common parent language which had since become extinct. He called the wider language family Indo-European, and the missing parent has since become known as Proto-Indo-European (PIE).

Some 40 years after Jones a German linguist by the name of Jacob Grimm, more famous as half of the Brothers Grimm, formulated three linguistic laws which explained how PIE had changed over time, eventually developing into modern Indo-European languages like German and English. The laws showed for example how the *pf* sound in German was related to the *p* in English, explaining how *pfund* and *pound* are linked. In doing so he helped account for the way PIE had evolved into all of the modern languages of the Indo-European group. Since the 19th century Grimm's laws have even been applied retrospectively, along with other linguistic scholarship, to reconstruct the missing PIE language.

For those keen to know how travel has always been part of our history there can be no more compelling evidence than the word 'journey'. A word that has links to the sky, to the landscape, to time and to our ancestral Gods. Journey preserves some of these links through the English word journal, 'events of the day', the Italian *giorno* and the French *jour*, both meaning day; and through the Latin word *diurnal*, 'daily', which by application of the relevant Grimm's law became the English word 'journal'.

Using Grimm's laws it has even been possible to reconstruct the missing PIE root word and to work forward from there. *Dyeu-s*, to our Indo-European ancestors, meant both sky and God and came from a root meaning 'to shine' or 'bright'. A meaning which records the sun as perhaps the original human deity and illustrates a shift away from the animistic traditions of the Paleo- and Mesolithic periods towards the Neolithic beginnings of monotheism.

It was at about this time, around 5000 BCE, that circles, probably representations of the sun, also appear in Man's art. And with the circles the first crosses appear. They are the equal-armed crosses that persisted into the Byzantine period and they come either separately or within the circle. To represent the four seasons, as these crosses may have, and the new deity *Dyeu-s*, the sun, together must have been a potent symbol to our ancestors.

Grimm's laws say that the word *Dyeu-s* developed into the *Zeus* of the Greek pantheon, also known as *Zeus pater*, 'father of the gods', who was *Jupiter* of the Roman period, often associated with the equal-armed cross within a circle.

The same symbol I saw at the museum in Ma'arat, carved into the creamy marble slabs lining the courtyard. There in front of me was Man's journey from nomad worshipping the sky, first to settled pagan farmer and then to urbanite worshipping the invented intellectual Gods of the new societies.

'These are *Chi-Rho* crosses,' Munif was saying, 'another early variation of the Christian cross.'

The cross in the circle was the shape of an X. In the left quadrant was the Greek letter *Chi* and on the right *Rho* (X and P respectively to modern eyes).

'They are the first letters of the Greek word *Christos*, meaning Jesus Christ.'

We took to the shadow of the colonnade, regrouping around another slab.

'This one has the Greek letters Alpha and Omega, the first and last letters of the Greek alphabet. This is something the new Christians took from the Jews, who said that God was the first and last of everything.'

Munif pointed to another circle carved into a piece of unblemished granite the colour of fresh milk.

'This one has everything. The circle and the vertical cross, the diagonals, *Chi-Rho* and Alpha and Omega.'

The X too was a Neolithic symbol, although ultimately Christianity would chose the upright cross, and later revise this to emphasise the symbolism of the crucifixion; but that afternoon in Ma'arat, baking beneath the high sun of the Syrian desert, Christianity's infancy was laid out to view.

We drove reluctantly back to the city, hot and happy like children returning from the beach. As the afternoon was to be my last in Syria, I made a friendly phone call to Ammar to say goodbye. Then for no other reason than there was credit left on the phone card, I called the Iranian embassy. To my delight and horror an overworked voice told me a visa had now been granted, could I pick it up tomorrow?

My Syrian visa had just two days remaining, which was just enough time to travel overnight by train to Damascus, collect the visa and get the bus back to Aleppo the following day. The internet travel agent through which I had applied for the visa even let me off paying because their website wouldn't accept my credit card. We agreed I would pay as soon as I entered Iran, and set a deadline of three weeks. I now had 21 days to get through Anatolia to the Iranian border, but as this was about what I'd planned anyway, it didn't seem a problem.

3

The Renaissance in
the Wilderness

Coryate left Aleppo in September 1614, having
had the good sense to wait until early autumn
for a caravan. By the time he left, any doubts about
his route had been banished. The caravan he joined
was bound for Esfahan, a thousand miles away to the
east in another world. For Coryate it was now the
Orient or bust. He was already resplendent in local
dress, with probably even a turban, and had been
away from home for two years. He had survived The
Turk, the pilgrimage to Jerusalem and the Syrian
desert; now he set himself the even sterner task of
walking to India.

From this point onward there would be no easy
way out. His route inland left behind any possibility
of a passing ship and there were no other Europeans
he could turn to for help before India. And neither, in
practice, could he leave the caravan once he had joined
it. To travel through Turkey or across the abandoned

wastes of Persia alone was suicide for locals let alone a single unprotected Christian. And even with the protection of a caravan, safety was far from guaranteed.

The further east Coryate went the further he penetrated a world of 17th-century myth and mystery. A world known at home only through rumour and the sketchy accounts of four English merchants who had so far been this way, one of whom died in the process; or known through caricature in plays like Marlowe's *Tamerlane* or Shakespeare's *Othello*. This was a time when maps really did bear that terrifying and credulous inscription 'here be dragons', or similar claims designed to hide a lack of geographical knowledge. Sometimes these claims could be strangely specific as well, as with one 15th-century map which describes 'men having large horns four feet long, and there are serpents also of such magnitude that they can eat an ox whole'. Finally, and perhaps most tellingly, some maps simply warn of elephants, hippos or lions.

Seen against a background of such comparative ignorance Coryate's courage is nothing short of remarkable. His was a world where the unicorn still existed (he reported seeing two in India – they were rhinos), where witches were real and where a ship might still sail off the edge of the world. It was the age of the leech, of thirteen devils on stage, of heresy and the Inquisition. Where Protestant and Catholic hated each other enough to tear Europe apart, yet the sight of a Muslim bought instant reconciliation.

～

There was only one modern border crossing between Syria and Turkey, near Aleppo, and so I was obliged to take it and deviate from Coryate's route for a few days. He went north-east while I went north, our routes converging in Birecik, a small Turkish town beside the Euphrates famous in antiquity as Zeugma, the last outpost of the Roman world.

Despite this being one of the most significant archaeological sites in Turkey, no one could tell me exactly where it was when I arrived in Birecik. It was not in town, that I knew, and several people I asked recognised the name, and agreed it was nearby, but couldn't tell me exactly where. And when I asked the hotel manager, he locked himself in his office, put the paper over his face and went to sleep.

In fact very little attention was paid to Zeugma until the 20th century, mainly because it was covered with pistachio trees. Even then it was not discovered deliberately but when some of the trees were cleared for farming, though as is too often the case, looters made the first discoveries. In the years that followed several irreplaceable mosaics, not to mention numerous artefacts, went missing before archaeologists were alerted.

It was as I was asking around that I met an urbane man called Üzgen in the large tin shed that passed for the town's market. It was the middle of the afternoon and the market was one of the few places that was still busy. Üzgen was a mechanic by trade and had worked in West Berlin for ten years before reunification. He returned to set up his own business and had fond memories of his time abroad, which had left him with the German 'obsession with cleaning'.

'Things are so dirty here', was the first thing he said. He was wiping mud from his carrots onto the outside of the bag they came in. 'And this man is too expensive. We have many farms around here but they only produce tobacco and pistachios, not vegetables. These', tapping the bag, 'come by truck from somewhere else. It's not far but it puts the price up'.

We adjourned to a *çayhane* (teahouse) that had been inserted into one sweltering corner of the market. A brass samovar was squirting steam against the corrugated wall and an old man in a crumpled suit was asleep on one of the benches. I noticed a couple of delicately embroidered ornamental cushions on a chair nearby and so while Üzgen sugared his tea, I slipped them onto the bench and sat on them, the trials of the long-distance cyclist being what they are.

Üzgen said he was in his fifties but he looked younger. He was well dressed and in this rough and ready bazaar town he was smart enough to be the mayor. He had acquired his dress sense in Germany, he said, where good clothes were easy to find, unlike Turkey where they grew good cotton but didn't produce anything fashionable. There were rules in Germany, he said distantly, gazing at the piles of vegetables laid out on trestles. As a mechanic he noticed them, in Health and Safety for example. That was a big problem in Turkey. Sure, there was supposed to be a Health and Safety Board, and there were supposed to be inspections, but in reality the regime was lax. You could cut corners in every walk of life, particularly building regulations. It was easy to build illegally, but Turkey was a major earthquake zone and the result was almost always bad. Out in the sticks people got away with things and Üzgen didn't like that. 'Sometimes bad people take advantage.' He raised his hands in exasperation like a waiter without plates. 'They want to make things cheaper for themselves – but you must follow rules.'

'I am a good man', he said and slurped his *çay*.

I had some sympathy with people who wanted to

make Turkey cheaper. Even compared with Britain some things were expensive. Petrol for one, which I couldn't help noticing because petrol stations were little patches of heaven for cyclists, complete with restaurants, tea shops, fresh water, ice cream and sometimes even carpets to snooze on. In some parts of Anatolia a litre of petrol cost the same as it did in London, a price that seemed unsustainable set against government salaries as low as £200 a month.

Üzgen put his glass down with a rattle. I would want to see the *Baraji*, he said confidently, the recently-built dam a few miles upriver on the Euphrates. It was part of Turkey's GAP (Anatolian irrigation) project, the largest water related project in the world and something he was obviously proud of. The dam would make it easier for people to farm here, Üzgen said, and – putting on an expression of practised sincerity – 'wealthy people are happy people'. Many of them went to the *Baraji*, for 'health sports', he continued, and suggested we go there for a swim.

At that moment, sitting beside a samovar, next to a metal wall that was humming with heat, in a dusty town at the top of the Mesopotamian plain, a swim was the single most sublime idea imaginable.

'I have a car.' said Üzgen. 'Mercedes. It is imported.' He twisted to wave at the waiter. 'But first, you are my guest so – more *çay.*' He ordered, then punched a number into his mobile phone, jabbing at the keypad as though reprimanding a child. He was calling his brother, he said, to make sure the car was free. A man came past and spoke to Üzgen, who dismissed him brusquely. The man was replaced by another dealt with in the same off-hand manner. Perhaps he was the mayor.

I went to my hotel 50 yards away for my towel and swimming trunks. When I came back there were two more glasses of tea on the table but no Üzgen. The waiter mimed another phone call and so I drank my tea and waited. Half an hour later I paid and stood outside blinking in the sunlight. When Üzgen didn't come I walked along the road, past a contorted bolt of rock that was the ancient citadel, past a shop selling tractors, past a tatty children's playground to a dusty teagarden beside the Euphrates. After another half an hour, and more *çay*, I went for lunch in a nearby restaurant.

It was only when I stood to leave that I realised Üzgen had been sitting a few tables away. He looked vaguely flustered in his loud shirt and pressed trousers and was staring hard at a menu. Beside him sat a matronly woman with a ruddy face and brown hands. She was wearing a full black *chador* and looked as rustic as Üzgen did urban. I thought she must be very proud of him, the local man who had made it abroad to Berlin; to a world of Deutschmarks and cleanliness, imported cars and better clothing. Set against this the woman seemed to personify what he had left behind.

As Üzgen could not have failed to notice me I couldn't resist a parting shot, just to let him know.

'Give my regards to your mother'. I nodded toward the woman and walked out.

'Wife.' Came Üzgen's terse reply from behind me. 'My wife'.

⤾

From Birecik Coryate walked east for two days to Urfa, which he called 'Ur of the Chaldeans' to distinguish it from Ur of the Babylonians further south, near Basra in modern Iraq. Both places claimed to be the birthplace of the Old Testament prophet Abraham, and this along with the linguistic similarity might explain why some historians had placed Coryate in Iraq for part of his journey.

Urfa was an ancient and elegant place, a cultural oasis in the Mesopotamian desolation that still felt significant. The city's notability has perhaps declined since its founding by Seleucis Nicator, one of the generals who succeeded Alexander the Great (and who also founded Zeugma). A little homesick, Nicator named the city Edessa after the Macedonian capital he had left. The Urfalees see this date as the end of ancient history and the beginning of civilisation.

In 190 CE, through the conversion of its King Abgar IX, the city had become the first Christian state, more than 100 years before Armenia and also before Constantine's Edict of Milan of 313 CE, banning the persecution of Christians. By the early 3rd century Edessa was one of the foremost cities in the Christian world with a sizeable religious community and a flourishing scriptural tradition. Her monks were among those in the ancient Christian world who translated not only religious texts – from Greek into their lingua franca, Aramaic – but also the most popular scientific works of the day. The geometry of Euclid, the medical works of Galen and Hippocrates, the philosophy of Aristotle and Plato. All were translated during this period in Edessa, and at other places in the region, and preserved in the libraries as a matter of religious duty.

When the Umayyad dynasty, the first wave of Muslim expansion outside Arabia, extended its dominion in the 7th century, Edessa was engulfed. Initially the speed of that expansion meant local administration was retained and government carried out mainly by proxy. Monasteries and other Christian institutions were not generally troubled and in fact sometimes benefited from Muslim interest. Edessa's scriptoria, like others in the area, were used for the translation of those same scientific texts, this time from Aramaic into Arabic. Once translated, Islamic scholarship used the knowledge as a basis from which to develop its own well-known excellence in mathematics, geometry and medicine, among other fields. The final stage in this journey of knowledge saw Europe rediscover and adopt much classical learning, often from the translations of Arabic and Persian scholars. Men like al-Kwarizmi, whose name was romanised to algorithm, and whose method for solving equations, *al-jebr*, gave us 'algebra'; and Ibn Sina, romanised to Avicenna, whose *Canon of Medicine* was part of the foundation of modern medicine. In this way improved versions of the old 'Greek knowledge' came back to a world which had spurned them in favour of Iconoclasm and the Inquisition. The circle was complete, from the classics to the Renaissance via Aramaic, Arabic and Persian; from classical Greece to Christian Europe via the Muslim Middle East.

In the early centuries of Christianity priests also travelled further east from Edessa setting up a Persian church, which along with the church in Edessa was later declared Nestorian, and therefore heretical. Edessa's church was closed by the Roman emperor Zeno in 488 CE and many Edessan Christians went to Persian Nisibis nearby. Persian emperors – embroiled in centuries' old conflict with Catholic Rome – looked more kindly on them once they were there, even installing a Nestorian as bishop at the expense of the existing, Catholic, bishop, who was executed.

In modern Urfa this Christian heritage had largely been forgotten in favour of the later legend of Abraham, whom both Islam and Christianity revere as the first prophet. Urfa's legend of Abraham centred on the two ornamental lakes in the sumptuous old quarter of town, and on two columns that were the sole remnants of the citadel above. Abraham had angered the local pagan deity Nimrod, the story went, who imprisoned him as punishment. The cruel Nimrod then decided to dispose of Abraham by using the pillars as a catapult and flinging the hapless prophet onto a pyre in the city below. Seeing his servant so dealt with God intervened, turning the fire into water and the embers into carp. From then on the city has maintained the two pools and their fish as sacred. No one may eat the carp, the legend says, or they will be struck blind as punishment. Consequently the lakes teem with very well-fed fish.

Coryate knew of the city's association with Abraham because he spent four days searching for the house where he was born, although he 'could see no part of the ruins of the house where that faithful servant of God was born, though I much desired it.' The problem may have been that Coryate was searching for a house, when apparently Abraham had been born in a cave. This at least is how the story was told in modern Urfa. A relatively large cave, too, nestling beneath the robust ridge where the citadel and its now forlorn pillars stood.

A mosque had been built close to the cave's mouth and a colonnade extended a proprietorial arm along the rock face. The entrance was covered by the colonnade's delicate arches and a wooden cabin with separate entrances for men and women. Through that segregated doorway the entrance to the cave itself was so low that you had to crouch to get into the tiny antechamber. Here a window overlooked the cave, though access was limited to mosque staff. Turkish visitors peered into the gloom through a smeared window, talking in whispers about what the prophet might conceivably have done in the cave. As a mark of respect they preferred not to turn their backs as they left, creating the incongruous sight of many trousered bottoms squirming backwards into the sunlight.

When I left Urfa the temperature went up. The two days it took to reach Diyarbakir were through a furnace of the most inhospitable wilderness I had ever seen. The world became a kind of geologist's fantasy in which every feature of the landscape had been replaced by rock. Gentle slopes were peppered not with trees but with boulders, and around each boulder a corona of rubble like shrubs, and in the space between where grass should have been there was only a carpet of round pebbles, like geological condensation.

Each curve in the road led not around or past this surreal place, but deeper into it, and ultimately across it. Thousands of acres burnt to a crisp, scoured by the incessant desert wind; blown into flattened, threadbare hills where slabs of rock the colour of molasses lay as though placed for display.

Neither was there any shade anywhere along the way. Nor any traffic, either by some coincidence or design − as it seemed to my lightly steamed brain − and the combination was intimidating. I ploughed on through the swimming miasma of heat as the rocky world wobbled in a mute, mocking parody. In Sivarek, a mean little Kurdish town where I spent the night, I passed a man cramming a goat into the boot of his car and thought I'd gone mad. His wife was buying a hurricane lamp and was paying with salt.

Not far from Sivarek I got my first glimpse of the mountain that dominated the area, the Karacadag or 'Black Mountain', the only vertical thing in the landscape larger than a telegraph pole. Once a volcano, the Karacadag had covered a hundred square miles with basalt, colouring the landscape dark brown. The mountain was visible from perhaps 20 miles away and all I could do was cycle towards it, knowing from the map that I would have to cross its flanks. As I sat thinking about this, measuring each pedal stroke to save the energy I would need, the medieval phrase 'the prisoner is shown the instruments of torture' slipped into my mind and began circulating like a sadistic mantra. Then the world tilted, rolled back like an aircraft taking off and for two hours I rode uphill without a single thought. At one point I sought some shelter by laying in a gully like a soldier under fire, but even here the sun forced me on.

Unable to escape physically my mind did the only thing it could and went elsewhere.

That is me now, a tiny speck far below crawling through the Anatolian wilderness, visible only as a void of shadow in a blinding eternity. A human vacuum sucking down heat, cycling forever along an earthbound flight path into nothingness. The land around me is the colour of ancient bones, each rock welded to the ground below by the passing aeons. I sit all day never moving in a landscape that is squashed flat beneath a pristine and breathless sky. I do nothing. I'm just there, on the steppe, existing.

Then I was in Diyarbakir, suddenly, sweeping along a chaotic road lined with people on an ordered pavement beside shops and offices. The emptiness of the desert was over, replaced by its opposite, an unabashed city full of angles and lines that chequered the strong light into variegated shadow.

I didn't stop until I had passed through the ancient walls and was safe inside the old city. In Diyarbakir life somehow went on as normal, as though the desert outside didn't exist. People did their shopping, drove their cars, chatted in restaurants. But I found a hotel and cowered there, glad of the protection.

The two days from Urfa had changed things. Diyarbakir had been made different by the effort it took to get there. Skewed from reality, so that like the medieval mariners, and in fact like Coryate when he crossed the Euphrates at Birecik, I felt I had gone over the edge.

Out in the trickling heat, beyond the ramparts, the land fell away steeply into the great valley of the

Tigris. Dusty fields, flashes of green and scrubby vegetation stretched out in a great curve between teetering river banks 100 feet high. From the wall I could see Diyarbakir's low Byzantine bridge crossing the wide river bed, its gently pointed arches carrying the Silk Road into barbarian lands. On the walls I was in Mesopotamia; in front of me in the haze across the Tigris was the Orient, the unknown outside the classical world that had so frightened and enthralled everyone from the Greeks onwards. I was at the furthest edge of knowledge, of what Coryate, with his classical education and religious upbringing, would have known about or could have guessed at. This was the point at which the maps ended and the dragons began. Ever since the Greeks, and later the Romans, fought the Persian empires of their day, all that happened out in the Orient had been beyond control, beyond comprehension and beyond caring.

﹀

Diyarbakir's old city was locked inside three solid miles of basalt wall secured by a string of fat watchtowers like black pearls. It sat on the back of a bony escarpment that made the towers into a kind of malevolent toothy grin. Here and there some of the wall was ragged, and a couple of short sections were missing, but essentially this was the wall built in the Byzantine period by Constantius II to keep out Persian and Muslim armies. It was also the same wall Coryate saw, its reputation drawing visitors even then. His caravan would have camped beside the Tigris where there was space to feed and water the animals. Diyarbakir was a significant staging-post in the journey east as it was here that camels were swapped for horses and mules, which were more sure footed in the mountainous country to come.

It was on these black walls, with Coryate no doubt sightseeing, that a serious misfortune overtook him. As he marvelled at the city's grandeur he was interrupted by a *spahi*, a kind of knight or feudal landowner. A *spahi* could be called up to fight in defence of the Empire, and this combined with their domestic duties meant they usually went about heavily armed. Standard equipment was a long lance, a stout bow with a quiver of short arrows and a single-handed scimitar. Cornered by such a man the conventional wisdom was to do exactly what he said, so when this particular *spahi* demanded Coryate hand over his money, that is what he did, losing a good deal of his hard-earned cash.

This was a serious blow to the perennially broke Coryate, who was managing to live on just a few pence a day as he travelled. Although he seems to have had the last laugh because whatever the guard took, he didn't get everything. Like any sensible traveller Coryate had more than one stash, which is to say that although he was carrying all of his money, it wasn't all in the same place. Coryate still walked away with some gold and silver coins hidden 'in certain clandestine corners', as he tactfully puts it in one of the letters. He doesn't mention this method of banking anywhere else, so it was either done with foresight that morning or with eye-watering stoicism every day.

⌒

On my way back from trekking around the walls I came across a middle-aged man in an alleyway, sitting on a step hugging his knees like a disaffected teenager. He was sallow faced with silver hair and a slightly sheepish expression. He waved to me as I passed and dragged a large set of keys out of his pocket, proudly displaying a motif enamelled on a bright yellow fob. He came closer so that our heads almost touched as we examined the black papal cross in the centre. He was Christian, he said, checking my face, one of the few left in the city.

By way of encouragement I asked if he knew the Chaldean church. I'd gone into the old town hoping to find this church because it was one of a few that still clung to life in this region, and because it was also – just conceivably – a place Coryate visited. I said I would be grateful if he could direct me there but the man seemed to have other ideas. He gave an 'I can do better than that' smile and set off at a jog into the fractured streets.

I went after him dodging detritus between ratty two- and three-storey townhouses that pressed together in medieval proximity. Here and there children played unattended in alleyways and the occasional dog slunk past just out of thrashing range.

At the end of a series of ever narrower alleys we arrived in front of a locked iron gate. This, said the man producing the keys again, was the church of St Cyriacus, the Chaldean Catholic church. He was its caretaker.

The church itself was no longer used, the man said, as we crossed the baking courtyard. The building had partially collapsed and was dangerous so services were held in the presbytery next door, a simple, non-committal place like a sanctified village hall. The caretaker ushered me inside and we sat in the cool for a moment recovering from the heat.

I wanted to know something about the church's history and asked what he knew. In response he launched into what was obviously a well-rehearsed lecture, which he seemed about to deliver anyway. It was important, he said, that I understood why this church was here. He nodded thoughtfully in confirmation that a lecture was indeed required. It would explain why the Chaldean church was 'unique'.

After Christianity first diverged in the 5th century, he said, the Middle East went on to became part of the Eastern Orthodox church (as opposed to the Western, Catholic rite). Within eastern Orthodoxy different locations soon began to follow differing paths. The church in this part of Turkey was known as the Assyrian church because the area was ancient Assyria, though the language of the litany was Syriac, a form of Aramaic, rather than Assyrian. He saw me scribbling and waited. The Assyrian church waxed and waned for a thousand years or more until it too split in the 16th century. The caretaker moved his hands apart in a theatrical fashion. Thereafter one of the two schisms allied itself to Rome and became the Chaldean Catholic church, today based in Baghdad with an archbishop in Diyarbakir (although he currently lives in Istanbul).

'This is that church'. The man held his arms out. He was sure, he said, nodding in encouragement, that I now saw the church's strength. It was the only church that united Eastern and Western traditions, the Orthodox and Catholic sacrament that had anathematised each other in the 11th century and had so far failed to reconcile. But here – arms wide – that split no longer existed. This was one big happy family. He looked at me levelly while I took in the empty pews and the one or two icons on a makeshift altar.

'Now,' he said importantly, 'do you have any questions for me?'

Missing his point entirely, I lost no time in asking about Coryate. Did the church have any records going back perhaps to the 17th century, possibly even the year 1614. The site dated to 1624 according to an inscription over the door but it was just possible that some documents had been preserved.

'You see I'm looking for an Englishman who might have come here,' I went on hopefully. 'He came to the city for sure, in October 1614, and he spent at least one day here ...'

Perhaps if the church itself had no record then the priest of the day may have made some sort of personal account.

'It would have been very unusual for a Christian from Europe to come here, so it's possible some mention was made in the records. The man's name was Thomas Coryate.'

My babbling had confused the caretaker and he fell silent. Perhaps he was recalling some nugget of information, some key fact remarkable enough to have been locked away for years in his memory ready for just such an occasion.

He meandered over to the back wall and stood beside an ill-assorted group of bright and childish paintings.

'Thomas Coryate ...', he said slowly, 'Thomas Coryate ... yes, I know the name.'

'You've heard of him!' I squeaked, trotting after him. 'I can't believe it, you've actually heard of him, that's fantastic.'

The caretaker looked pleased at my reaction, then shot me an on-and-off smile and took a breath. To my surprise we were moving on.

'This church is very old,' he said, 'and the Chaldean church is the only Catholic church in Turkey.' It was difficult to get help from the government because the church was an import from the West. Eastern Christianity was given more respect, he said, but the Chaldean church was being neglected.

'Building work is expensive and the church cannot pay its staff: I am just a volunteer.'

The Orthodox church of St Mary nearby had the draw of a famous relic, he added sadly, in the form of the Apostle Thomas' bones, brought back from India in the 3rd century. Here – shaking his head – they were not as lucky.

There was a pause and I held my breath for something more about Coryate.

'But we have a large congregation and it is an active church so we need many donations. The congregation is 50; sometimes even 100.'

He continued talking, telling me that there were just fifteen Assyrian families left in Diyarbakir now, whereas before the First World War there had been 600. Most of the Christians in the area had died or left since that time; those who remained were mostly Orthodox, although they sometimes came here to worship. But I had already lost interest. I wanted to hear about Coryate from this man who knew his name. A man who worked in a church Coryate might have visited, who might just have access to exactly the kind of records I was looking for, if such records existed.

When he didn't go back to the subject I stopped him in mid sentence.

'I'm sorry, but would you mind telling me more about Thomas Coryate? How did you come to hear his name?'

The man looked at me peevishly. He shuffled his feet and gazed at the ceiling.

'Thomas Coryate,' he said vaguely, 'Thomas Coryate.' His brow twisted into to a frown. 'When is he arriving?'

I actually did groan. Although I must also have continued behaving in a relatively normal way because the man went back to his speech. Because the church was so poor he was forced into a commercial endeavour. These paintings, for example, were by his daughter and they were for sale. His daughter was an artist who sold paintings in Istanbul. People who came to the church had bought them in the past, he said. An American lady who visited last year bought three.

I hated them. I felt foolish. The church had been tainted by the caretaker's exaggeration and by my own naiveté. Suddenly I couldn't stay longer. I made an excuse and left, but the caretaker followed me out into the courtyard, abandoning the paintings in favour of straightforward begging.

'Just a few dollars ...' His plaintive voice drifted after me in the stifling air. 'Don't you have any money for me?'

Embarrassed and angry I growled over my shoulder: 'No I don't, but I'll tell Thomas Coryate to give you some when he gets here.'

4

Armenia the Lesser

The Ulu mosque's black basalt courtyard was softened to textured grey by the mid-day sun. A couple of Kurdish men in old suits moved listlessly across the paving towards the mosque, a square two-storey building making up one side of the courtyard. I had already been inside enjoying the cool, ancient and angular solidity of the building. The prayer hall was carpeted and divided lengthways by a series of tall buttresses, and except for the marble *minbar* (pulpit) against one wall, there was little decoration.

Now I was squinting in the Anatolian sun outside, not because the interior was in any way dull but much more because the mosque's most striking feature by far was in that blazing courtyard.

Buried in the centre of Diyarbakir's old city, the mosque was interesting in its own right, being just about the first Muslim building of any size outside Arabia. But what made it unique was a series of columns running around the walls of the courtyard, pacing out the walls and setting up a rhythm in petrified history.

The columns came originally from the 7th century cathedral of St Thomas, which had been built on the same site. Each one was decorated with geometric detailing from top to bottom; patterns that seemed to fit into no category I was familiar with. And neither was their heritage obvious in any later or modern architecture I could bring to mind. The columns almost seemed to stand outside time, an evolutionary dead end fossilised in the dry Anatolian air. One column was completely covered with a spiralling rhomboid swastika interspersed with acanthus leaves; an italicised swastika mingled with a flower like a Tudor rose and spiralled down another; a third was covered with Byzantine crosses linked geometrically so that swastikas formed in the interstices; while yet another was embossed with a simpler slanting diamond. And to finish the tableau each column was capped with a gorgeously ornate Corinthian capital like an inverted meringue.

Unfortunately for the cathedral the Umayyad expansion of the 7th century reached Diyarbakir in 639 CE, just ten years after it had been built. The building remained intact for several centuries afterwards, although dual worship began immediately. Ultimately the cathedral would be rebuilt as a mosque after an earthquake in the 11th century meaning that, with the notable exception of the pillars, the cathedral was lost to the passage of time.

Those unexpected swastikas were another Indo-European symbol that emerged with the first crosses after the last ice age. They seem to have been a good luck charm of sorts and their use by religions such as Jainism, Hinduism and Buddhism, as well as the Roman army, follows this pattern. As decoration on the columns those distorted swastikas and the other slurred designs seemed almost to come from a previous version of Christianity, something unfamiliar and alien to someone from the West. Almost another religion.

It was a pity that Coryate did not seem to have visited the mosque. He would certainly have had something to say about it, whether it was to marvel at the beauty of the columns or to rant at the loss of the cathedral. In fact it may have been difficult for him, or any other Christian, to visit the mosque at the time. By the early 17th century Islam had become the main social and political influence from North Africa to Calcutta, and the enlightened days of dual worship at places like the Ulu mosque were long over. Most of Islam's sacred places were now its own.

If Coryate did get to see inside the Ulu mosque he would have undoubtedly enjoyed the experience. So much so that he might have been observed walking up and down the prayer hall with unusual concentration, almost as though meditating. He had been in the habit of measuring the buildings he visited on his European trip by the simple method of pacing them out. Not every building was suitable of course, those with obstructions like pews, or any with semicircular plans were difficult, but he gives them a go, faithfully recording width and breadth in multiples of his own stride. The interlocking squares and oblongs of the Ulu mosque, and indeed most Muslim buildings, would have been perfect for such an *ad hoc* survey and it is hard to believe that Coryate did not continue his habit here.

While this may sound like an exaggeration, Coryate's status as one of the few Englishmen abroad at the time gave him a certain latitude. In the 17th century England was enjoying a vogue for all things Italian, especially if they were Venetian; Venice then being that weird and dangerous concept in pre-Civil War England, a republic. To those at home even something as basic as the dimensions of Piazza San Marco would have been of interest.

The *Crudities* was a mixture, in this way, of the high- and low-minded written in a sometimes pompous, sometimes workman-like fashion. Always empirically driven, the *Crudities* was also rather advanced. Despite the odd rant at the follies of Papism, the book reveals an innate interest in all things foreign and in a similar way Coryate's Asian journey was playing to a nascent English interest in the Orient. At a time when for most people the myth and fact of 'abroad' could live quite happily in their minds, Coryate was abroad seeing it for himself. In the circumstances even the simple act of a describing a mosque's dimensions could be immensely useful. To make something better known is always to make it less frightening, and giving a mosque real-world proportions would have helped even The Turk become human.

Coryate's European trip had qualified him by experience for his job, and given him the 'tools' he needed to analyse his world, although this approach bought a certain amount of mockery from many of his contemporaries. 'Tombstone traveller', they christened him for his habit of transcribing epitaphs and inscriptions. Some saw his book as boring and its length and tone self-indulgent. As a consequence it received very little serious praise when it was published. Instead Coryate received a much fuller measure of general ridicule.

John Donne gives a further clue as to why *Crudities* was not immediately recognised as the milestone it was. ''Tis no one thing', he says in his poem *Upon Mr Thomas Coryat's Crudities*, 'it is not fruit nor root.'

As this line shows, the readership had to contend with the question of what genre the book was. It was not a guidebook, which in any case did not exist then in the modern sense; neither was it a treatise on, for example, European architecture, though it contained screeds of detail on the subject; it was not a moral tale and it was not an anthropological study, though it is full of the custom and colour Coryate encountered along the way.

In fact the book was a mish-mash of all of these. Fable, anecdote, analysis, eulogy, character vignette, petty revenge and self-justification. Perhaps it came closest to memoir, though because it described no momentous events – concentrating often on the mundane – it had the ring of something perhaps less worthy. Travel writing is many things, and has become many more things over the centuries, all of which were found together, for the first time, in Coryate's book. As a consequence, and as Donne's poem suggests, *Coryat's Crudities* was unclassifiable.

I liked the Ulu mosque because that too stood outside the norm. And for me it was wholly new. Christianity and Islam combining, symbolically, in an architectural expression of their relationship.

Coryate's caravan crossed the River Tigris at Diyarbakir and walked beside the river for several days
before turning northwards. From here it wound its
way up the precarious Bitlis valley into the Torosular
mountains, then on across a stunted brown plateau to
Tatvan, at 5,577 feet, on Lake Van. Having left the
Mesopotamian plains behind the world would now
be one of mountains and the elevated rocky deserts
of the Iranian plateau that went on all the way to the
Mughal Indian border.

The caravan would have taken to the southern
shore of Lake Van before turning inland through a
range of beige hills that were piled against each other
like sacks of grain. Once through the hills the road
rejoined the lakeshore, arriving several days later in
the city of Van.

The area around Van had been hotly disputed
since before Roman times and slaughter was still
a way of life during Coryate's era. One of the very
few Englishmen who used this route before him, a
Reverend John Cartwright, reported that his caravan
was attacked five times before reaching the safety of
Persia. Robert Coverte, another Englishman, who
made the journey from India to Aleppo with a com-
patriot in 1610, was robbed so many times that he

arrived in Aleppo with nothing but his clothes and the camel he rode on.

Ottoman law often prevailed in name only outside the walled towns, and most governors lacked the resources and inclination to go chasing Kurdish tribesmen across the steppe. In any case caravans still had to pay their dues at the towns, whether they had been robbed or not, so there was little incentive to waste men and money protecting them.

I was able to follow Coryate's route up off the Mesopotamian plateau, through the Bitlis valley to Bitlis itself, where I slept in a tiny wooden restaurant overhanging the thundering river. Tatvan, which stood at the railhead for the train to Iran, was almost comically full of restaurants and hotels. Every day passengers embarked here for the ferry ride along the lake, then joined the onward service in Van. The city was well used to visitors but had a strained, temporary jollity that somehow made everyone on the streets look like refugees.

After the hills Van was a welcome splash of colour, or at least a welcome absence of beige. The angles and changing focuses were restful to the eye too, although without the road constantly disappearing beneath the front wheel there was a strange optical illusion of the world receding. This later turned into a splitting headache, and I was forced to spend an unplanned day in Van. I spent the time at the ancient citadel beside the lake and in the evening went on a kind of cake pub crawl, systematically working through all of the cafés near my hotel. Then, currency happy at the approaching border, I ate a sumptuous evening meal in the best restaurant I could find.

⌒

Away from the city fresh green hills drew up on either side of the road and the valley began to close in. Fields appeared, planted with vegetables and grain where in Mesopotamia they had been dust. There were even stands of conifer here and there, and in the grass below, delicate papery flowers swayed like kelp at the water's edge. The road continued in this mockingly pleas-ant fashion, then rose again through a thin pasture of lush grass to a small pass – which was where things started to go wrong. The rush from Diyarbakir to Van had been sapping and a single day's rest nowhere near enough. I had made good progress against the visa deadline, but now I was paying for it.

In the darker moments of the next few hours the thought of not making it to India lingered in the shadows. Surat seemed such a long way away and already things were difficult. Coryate talked of how he had been in the best of health for the whole of his walk, and suffered only three days of fever in Constantinople. Just to emphasise that he was travelling in the 17th century, the fever was, 'with a little letting blood clean banished'. For the remainder of his journey he enjoyed, 'as sound a constitution of body and firme health as ever I did since I first drew this vitall ayre'. A year later in India he was still in rude health, reporting in one of the letters that, 'I do enjoy at this time as pancraticall and athleticall a health as ever I did in my life.'

Half an hour later I was at the top of a ridge looking down into the Kurdish village of Hosap and the broken remains of the most magnificent castle. The outer wall covered most of the hillside and in places was remarkably intact. The keep rose straight from a broken stack of rock beside the road, towering over the bazaar below in a proprietorial way. The castle was built in the mid-17th century by a Kurd named Sari Suleiman the Blond, a warlord about whom not one kind word was ever written. The broken teeth of the walls and the amputated stack of rock below were perfect for such a man; even 400 years later the castle positively glowered over the valley beyond.

But it wasn't the castle that made Hosap memorable that day, it was failure. Here in the black shadow of the fortress I gave up the chase to the border, now down to its final day, and hitched a lift. I still had to cover 100 miles, climb a 6,500-foot pass, cross into Iran, find a bank and make the payment, all by five o'clock the following day. At my current pace it would take three days just to reach the border.

With a heavy heart I rode slowly out of Hosap. I stood beside the road, stuck out my thumb and to my great surprise had a ride within five minutes. In fact it was the first vehicle that passed, a grimy blue truck with a flapping tarpaulin like a torn spinnaker. The driver had an angular careworn face like a brown cashew nut and introduced himself as Muhammad; his assistant was Rashid. Neither of them spoke English, he said, but I was welcome in Turkey and welcome in their truck.

I put the bike in the back, where it joined various greasy sacks, tyres and other oddments. Then I climbed into the cab before anyone could change their minds.

Muhammad wanted to make the most of this opportunity with a foreigner and was soon miming questions to me. How did my bicycle pump work, he wanted to know – just like a Turkish one; where did I get that T-shirt – actually, Istanbul; and where did I get such great shoes? Aha, he said when I answered this one, and my glasses too, they must also be from 'Engelstan'. He was shortsighted himself. Could see the dials all right – tapping the dashboard – but everything else was a blur. Could he try my glasses on?

I thought this was a bad idea, firstly because they would be the wrong prescription and secondly because I might not get them back anyway.

To change the subject I pointed to the wires hanging out of the dashboard – what happened there? Oh, you know, said Muhammad, you fix one thing and it leads to ten others.

But wasn't that the speedometer, I asked.

Yes, he roared, picking it off the floor, and it still was. He shoved it back into the dashboard and thumped Rashid. *It still was*.

We pushed on along the valley beyond Hosap with the road rising up across the shoulders of a ridge. Muhammad's phone rang and he passed it to Rashid. You answer it, he yelled, you know how deaf I am. Rashid dutifully took the phone and began relaying a message over the din. This proved to be quite a hardship for him as he had one of the most serious stammers I'd ever heard.

The truck wound deeper and deeper into the hills until, with a series of adenoidal gear changes, we came to the last and steepest section of the climb.

We all took hold of the cab to steady ourselves and were thrown against each other as a result. Muhammad said we should relax more and go with the flow, so we relaxed and were duly thrown against the cab instead. The speedometer popped out of the dashboard and landed on the floor with a thunk. It doesn't matter, Muhammad bawled, we're not going that fast anyway. He roared with laughter and thumped Rashid – *not going that fast*. Rashid tore his eyes away from the abyss below us and smiled feebly. Beside the road a flimsy crash barrier was now all that separated the truck, its short-sighted, deaf driver and his two rabbit-eyed passengers, from oblivion.

An hour later on the plateau we had gained, we came to Baskale, a small dusty town full of mud-brick walls and Italian cypress trees. On the outskirts Muhammad slowed the truck to a walk and began peering at several young boys beside the road. They seemed slightly embarrassed by this and shuffled their feet in the dust. Some, I noticed, were making furtive gestures at the passing traffic. Muhammad was rapt by these performances and pulled over beside one angelic lad with his hair scraped into a side parting. He chatted with the boy for a while until a bearded man appeared and took over the conversation. What he said seemed less to Muhammad's liking and so we drove on, though Muhammad kept his eyes on the side of the road as we went.

I couldn't help wondering what had just happened and so as the truck wheezed back up to speed I asked Rashid what was going on.

Oh that, he said laughing. We were just trying to buy fuel for the truck. Each of the boys was a front for the family petrol smuggling business, which they advertised using hand signals from the roadside. The boys were used because they looked innocent and because they were too young to charge if they were arrested. Once a driver stopped the father or an uncle took over negotiation. The price had seemed good at first but we would have had to buy a tank-full and Muhammad was reluctant.

After Baskale we drove on relentlessly. The afternoon's friendly banter dwindled and both men became ever more intent on the road. The sun set and an hour later we entered a narrow forested valley just as the last band of indigo was charred from the sky. The truck slowed and wobbled across the road coming to rest in the dust beside a collection of simple concrete buildings.

'Problem,' announced Muhammad climbing out. 'Problem' echoed Rashid following him into a squalid-looking restaurant. I climbed out into the deafening silence and stood beside the truck mildly stunned. There was the faint scent of pine on the air, which was at last cool, and overhead stars glittered in a clear sky. The odd light winked on the opposite side of the valley and in the distance the sound of goat bells mixed with the burble of a river.

I went into the restaurant, at a loss as to what to do. It seemed we were not going to Yuksekova, the last town before the border, after all. I went to Muhammad with a questioning expression.

It's OK, he said, we can go on in the morning, we'll be in Yuksekova in no time. To emphasise the fact that this wasn't a problem he and Rashid ordered dinner.

I knew I would have woken to fresh air, shaggy haystacks, patchwork fields: unmechanised farming in all its picturesque glory, but it was not to be. I had to push on. I tried to get Muhammad to tell me what the problem was, in case I could help. Was it the truck, had it finally konked out? Were we out of petrol? Or was it — I lowered my voice to ask — the PKK? Were they a danger here?

Abdullah Öcalan, the imprisoned leader of the PKK (the Kurdistan Workers' Party) had decreed a renewal of terrorist activities from his prison cell six weeks ago. We were now about as deep into Kurdish territory as it was possible to get, something that had been reinforced a few miles back when we passed a sign announcing Hakkari, the most distant and troubled of all Turkey's provinces. The northern Iraqi Kurdish zone, where Öcalan's fighters went to hide after the PKK's 1999 cease-fire, was just 30 miles to the south. There was even a convenient road for them to use if they wanted to return – this road.

Two other trucks pulled up in the darkness and half a dozen men clambered out. I dearly wanted to be in Yuksekova that night, both because I wanted to make Iran the following day and also because I didn't want to sleep on the restaurant's greasy floor. In desperation I unloaded the bicycle as a hint and made a final attempt with Muhammad. Had the PKK issued any threats recently? Were they were staging roadblocks?

Muhammad exploded. He slammed his glass down and looked at me furiously.

'It's not the PKK', he shouted, 'it's me, OK. I can't see to drive at night so we have to stop – is that all right with you? I'm old and I can't see properly just like I told you, so if you want to go tonight you'd better go with someone else.'

He waved a hand at the passing traffic. 'You're a guest here, anyone would be pleased to take a foreigner.'

He went back to what was left of his çay and eve-ryone sank into silence. I sat forlornly looking at my shoes for a while, then when conversation picked up I shuffled outside. I hid myself in the darkness and watched headlights sweep the valley wall opposite, then walked a little way along the road and stuck out my thumb.

This time the second vehicle stopped, a square van driven by two urbane Turks from Adana further west. At first they didn't see the bicycle and were making ready to leave when I pointed it out. The driver gave it a level stare and said, 'no problem', in English. He walked to the back of the van and opened the door onto a refrigerated compartment full of meat. I dragged the bike inside, much to his amusement, wedging it between a huge slab of beef and a crate of grinning goat heads.

As the man levered the door closed I took a last look back at the restaurant. An oblong of lurid yellow light framed the drivers and cut out into the inky night. Muhammad, his fleshy forehead and beaky chin like Mr Punch, was thumping one of the other truck drivers, telling a joke. Rashid was looking towards me, perched on a chair like a nervous Judy. I waved in salute and climbed into the cab.

Part II

PERSIA AND
THE SAFAVID EMPIRE

The Safavid dynasty (1502–1736) was a period of relative tolerance and cultural strength in Persia that saw the country's modern consciousness begin to take shape. It was during this period that Shia Islam came to prominence with Ismail I (r. 1502–24), who used Shi'ism as a means to strengthen Persian identity against neighbouring Sunni empires.

Persian art and literature underwent a resurgence, and Iranian culture enjoyed what is considered to be its finest artistic moment. Shah Abbas I (r. 1588–1629) is generally considered to be the greatest of the Safavid rulers, who apart from many other achievements founded the first carpet factory in Esfahan. This revitalised the industry and indirectly started the vogue for Persian carpets in the West.

Persia began trading directly with the new European powers at this time, notably Portugal, England and Holland while also continuing its historic role as a conduit for Silk Road trade. The craze for tulips and saffron that swept Europe in the 17th century was fed largely by availability of both flowers in Iran, where they are indigenous.

Trade also introduced Farsi (Persian) words like 'caravan' to English, where it joined 'checkmate', from *Shah maut*, 'the king is dead'. 'Arsenic', much favoured as a poison by royal families throughout the Middle East, also came into English as did 'turban' and 'rose'.

With new maritime routes to the East in the 17th and 18th centuries, overland trade with Persia began to decline. With it the Safavid dynasty began to crumble, helped by border squabbles and internal wrangling. The dynasty ended when the warlord Nader Shah, who had already conquered northern India, took the throne in 1736.

By the 20th century Western interest had shifted from trade to direct involvement, or rather interference. The attraction was now oil, a product that has had a defining influence on relations since. These relations became strained almost to breaking point after the Second World War when the West, mainly Britain and America, forced the then Shah from the throne in favour of his pro-Western son Reza Pahlavi, last of the Pahlavi dynasty.

The new Shah was to rule for almost 40 years, implementing a modernisation program that was so rapid it sometimes left much of the population behind (the country's name was changed to Iran at this time). Ever more dictatorial as the years went on, the Shah's rule finally ended with the 1979 revolution and the return of Ayatollah Ruhollah Khomeini from exile in a quiet Paris suburb. But the revolution he had advocated while still a figurehead of resistance, became progressively more religious as it gathered momentum. By the time Khomeini returned from Paris, Shia Islam was the revolution's sole identity and he its unchallenged leader.

Since his death in 1989 no changes have been made to the structure of government. Iran is still a theocracy in which ultimate power is vested in the Supreme Leader, currently Khomeini's hand-picked, and almost identikit, successor Ayatollah Khameini.

5

Dressing Up

By the time Coryate left England on his travels the country had already made a small number of contacts in the East. Perhaps the most notable was Sir Anthony Jenkinson, an Elizabethan adventurer and one-time ambassador to Moscow, who received the right to trade in Constantinople from Suleiman the Magnificent in the 1550s.

In 1599 the adventurers Anthony and Robert Sherley had come to Persia, again in the hope of trade. They were received by Shah Abbas who granted a *firmen*, a decree, in this case giving them the right to trade. Anthony Sherley was given the task of improving the Shah's army, although he returned home soon afterwards. Robert on the other hand stayed on considerably longer, eventually marrying the daughter of a local nobleman and rising to the status of ambassador. Keen to use this potential opportunity against the Ottoman Empire, Abbas sent him to Europe in an attempt to muster support. Unfortunately the proposed joint attack, in which Europe and Persia sandwiched the troublesome Turk, never materialised and in 1613 Robert Sherley returned empty-handed.

It was against this background that Coryate became the first independent Englishman to enter Persia as his caravan trudged east in the autumn of 1614. At the time north-west Persia was still undergoing the transition from Ottoman to Safavid rule and most of the area was a wasteland. So much of the landscape is still desert today that it was easy to imagine away the last 400 years. There were no crops because of the season, almost no wildlife because of the heat and very few villages. Where there was vegetation, an orchard or a productive field, the temperature meant that there was no one in them and so the landscape looked ravaged and bleak.

When Coryate came to Tabriz, he reported that Shah Abbas was then in Georgia consolidating his recent gains, or as Coryate put it, 'ransacking the poor Christians there with great hostility, with fire and sword'.

Abbas in fact counts as quite a reasonable man for the time. He was keen that the desolation his war with Turkey had created should not be repopulated, as habitation would have been helpful to an invading army. A lesser man would have slaughtered the popu-lace and kept the land clear by terror, whereas Abbas possessed a little more vision. He knew of the Arme-nians' reputation for trade and encouraged them to continue as Silk Road merchants. He even gave goods on account to encourage Armenian loyalty, which was especially important as he was relocating them to Esfahan, 600 miles away. Once there the new popula-tion was given land south of the city in what is now the suburb of New Jolfa, named after one of the deci-mated cities of the north. The Shah's gamble paid off and Armenian merchants subsequently became the mainstay of caravan routes through Persia, bringing in a great deal of wealth in the process.

Despite the Shah's enlightened attitude Tabriz was still in ruins when Coryate's caravan spent six days here. 'More woeful ruines of a city ... never did mine eies beholde', he says, deeply impressed. He goes on to quote Ovid to the effect that this can only be God making sport in human affairs.

The six-day layover may have been for a number of reasons. Perhaps there was a need to change the horses they had taken in Diyarbakir for camels once more. Tabriz was also the place at which the northern and southern trade routes through Turkey converged, and two caravans meeting here might have taken time to regroup or trade. There was also the possibility of trade in what was left of the Tabriz bazaar itself. Unfortunately again we are left to conjecture as Coryate left no detailed account of his time here; or rather the detailed account he undoubtedly made has been lost. He was at this time busily making his second set of notes, which he would leave in Esfahan, and so his letters from India give little information on what had happened up until then. Sadly it seems that Coryate was conscientiously saving everything for his forthcoming Great Book. A book that would have been a unique record of travel, and would have surely made its author a household name.

∽

In Tabriz I went into the first bank I came to, where I was finally able to pay for the visa that had been so kindly given in Syria, an event that was already a distant memory. The chasing about ended anti-climactically in the deputy manager's office with just one form and a single signature, after which we drank *chay* and chatted for 20 minutes.

Back in my hotel the day's pleasant tone continued when I came out of my room to the sound of female laughter from along the corridor. A voice called out, 'Are you a foreigner here?' A woman was leaning out of the room, and I couldn't put my finger on it, but there was something strange about her. It took a few seconds to realise that she wasn't wearing a *chador*.

I went to the room where the door was open to help with the heat, and peered in. The woman who had spoken, Sharin, was on a chair just inside the door a little like a sentry.

'I thought you were a foreigner,' she said smiling, 'I can usually tell.'

The room was full of women dressed in the kind of smart-casual clothing that European women might wear. Colourful clothing lay neatly on a dresser with ranks of shoes marshalled underneath. On a hat stand in one corner various *chadors* hung limply beside a couple of cotton frock coats. These garments – *chador* literally translates to 'tent' in Farsi – had been enshrined in law as part of Khomeini's revolutionary constitution. Women outside their homes now had to be covered except for the face, hands and feet. Everything else had to disappear. I had already seen small rebellions against this in the streets, where the younger women allowed the *chador*, or the scarves that some wore, to slip back a little from their hair. The coats, or *manteaux*, I saw here were the just-acceptable alternative interpretation of the modesty law, with women wearing them with trousers – usually jeans

– and a head scarf. During periodic summer crackdowns the *Mutaween* (the morality police) would send women home for dressing like this, after having given them a lecture on how good morals were worth more than personal comfort. The punishment could be as harsh as a $50 fine – half a month's salary – or two months in jail, depending on how bad a case of 'bad *hijab*' it was.

Seeing me dithering in the doorway, Sharin waved me in. The five women were sitting around the room in a kind of Iranian tableau of gentility, reading newspapers, sipping tea and chatting. They smiled beautiful, welcoming smiles and gazed at me almost expectantly. I became a little overwhelmed by this and was reduced to playing the role of The Englishman: 'How do you do? Delighted to meet you' and so on. The women squealed in delight and chorused their approval.

They were 'a kind of women's co-operative', Sharin said, a group of friends from Tehran who travelled together visiting the countryside during the holidays. One was a technician at Tehran University, another was a lecturer in German, another an administrator at Tarbiat Moallem teachers' university.

'We have come to visit Lake Orumiye on a health trip,' Sharin said. 'People often come here. They use the mud as medicine because it is good for things like rheumatism.' She mimed smoothing mud over her hips and knees.

'The salt makes it healthy – it is famous all over our country.'

I tried to stay at the door but Sharin insisted I go inside, although I did take the first chair available. The room was large and there were half a dozen chairs or sofas. On the floor was a magnificent Tabriz carpet, wine-red and intricately detailed with vines and interleaving floral patterns. I had never seen anything that so perfectly evoked Persian history and was surprised that most of it was covered by chair legs and suitcases.

Seeing that I looked a little uncomfortable Sharin dismissed my concern about the women's modesty. The Western media gave a false perspective, she said. 'It is what the television always says about us, isn't it. We are religious fanatics who live by stupid rules.' She frowned at me. 'But we are not like that – you will see. Anyway, there are only old women here,' she said mischievously, 'so you needn't worry.'

I protested at this in character, saying something about the room being filled with youth and beauty. There were more squeals and a bout of giggling.

'They want to know if you are married,' Sharin

said after a moment. 'In your country people don't get married so young I think. Not like here.' She lifted her chin to the window signifying Iran. 'If a woman is not married by 25 her friends think there might be something wrong. If she is not married by 30, she never will be.'

At that moment the manager appeared in the doorway and for a second I held my breath. But the man was so obsequious, and the women plied him with so many forceful questions, that I felt sorry for him. The man bowed to show he would do something about their requests then said a few words to Sharin.

'Ah, he says our bus is waiting,' she said waving him away. They were to be taken to the lake for their health visit. They were all looking forward to it and so they wanted to leave immediately, she said apologetically, but perhaps I would visit again later.

Intrigued by the women, and especially by their treatment of the manager, I resumed the walk I had been about to start to Saint Serkis church, south of the centre. It was part of the same Chaldean Catholic movement as the church in Diyarbakir and so, ever hopeful of finding something relating to Coryate, I went to see it.

The church was down an uneven alley full of printing presses and workshops. The ground smelt of urine and the clatter of machinery filled the air. The church

was tall and narrow, a classic Latin church with a cruci-
fix floor-plan. But where the proportions should have
generated a sense of scale, the result here was to under-
mine the building. Inside, the high ceilings emphasised the grubby cracking plaster, while the thick
white buttresses were almost completely plain. A few
small portraits in dark frames were all that softened
the stark interior. The altar too was simple and there
were so few pews that the church looked abandoned.

I was invited in by one of the church staff, a pale
middle-aged woman by the name of Jennifer whose
hands fluttered constantly to the cross at her neck. I
asked about the Chaldean Catholic church and she
said this was indeed it, although few people in Tabriz
knew that. Most Iranians were generally tolerant of
the church, which was to say that they didn't throw
bricks through the windows; but neither did they
appreciate the differences between this church and
any of the half-dozen others.

She was mournful. 'It's the history that matters.
People are only what their history is – if you confuse
these churches you can't understand the people who
belong to them.'

Christianity had a distinguished early history in
Persia and the woman's concern was for that, more
than for any particular church building. She wanted

these individual histories to continue, and also to know there was a place for her in one of them. She was almost dismissive of the building we stood in, saying simply that it served a purpose. I felt that she was embarrassed because the building was less than inspiring aesthetically. Perhaps also the pressure of being part of a minority caused her to view her surroundings differently; a form of escapism that evoked the glories of a longer, grander, history.

A history that is often dated to the first few years after Jesus' death when Christians, persecuted by Rome, were welcomed by the Persian Empire. For several centuries Christian groups were tolerated and even encouraged by the Zoroastrian state, until the picture changed dramatically in the 4th century. In 337 CE the Sassanid King Shapur II attacked the Byzantine Empire in an attempt to move Persian borders westwards. Many Persian Christians in Nisibis – now in modern Turkey east of Urfa – made the mistake of supporting Byzantium (later Constantinople) in the conflict. The campaign failed and in the resulting backlash Shapur ordered every Christian in Persian lands to be killed. Luckily 'only' around 15,000 of the 200,000 Christians died before Shapur followed them, and his successor discontinued the purge.

Soon afterwards the Persian church regrouped,

side-stepping the problem of allegiance with a formal split from the western church. In the second half of the 5th century the Persian church then strengthened its independence from Rome by welcoming the Nestorian Christians when Xeno's decree had ejected them from Edessa.

The woman's hands fluttered at her neck again. She was sorry that she couldn't speak English, she said, although I understood her perfectly, but if I could wait a couple of days the priest would come and his English was much better. At the moment he was visiting some of the 7,000 other Chaldean Catholics in north-west Iran, mainly scattered in the towns and villages between Orumiye and the Armenian border. She apologised for being disorganised but usually no one came here unless there was going to be a service.

To keep the conversation going I asked how old the church was, but the woman had already turned to leave and there was little to do but follow.

'Would there be any records from the 17th century? Perhaps there was an archive ... ?'

'Oh, no,' she said, 'everything was destroyed a long time ago. And when the Soviets came in after the Second World War many people destroyed their own records.' Most of the Christian population who had stayed in Tabriz survived in this way.

Jennifer saw me to the gate and I stepped back out into the alley. We chatted briefly and I thanked her. At the last moment she smiled. A sad, thankful smile, but a smile none the less. Then the door closed and I heard the bolt slide home.

From the church I walked north and east along wide shopping streets choked with traffic. Between the pavement and the road a gully of clear water added a civilising· touch and kept motorcyclists off the pavements, although during rush hour nothing could stop this menace.

I was looking for a place Jennifer had mentioned, the poet's tomb a mile from the centre, in the hope that it would somehow make up for missing Coryate at yet another church. What I eventually found was an enormous and blindingly white edifice of modular marble, a three-storey Meccano kit set in a huge formal garden and dedicated to some fifty poets. It was another of Iran's unashamedly modernist structures built on the unnecessarily large scale that was a reflection of the country's size rather than anything poetic. The fashion had begun during the last Shah's reign and was perhaps understandable in a place six times the size of Britain with only 10 per cent more people. Space was a natural resource in Iran and the habit of scale had become ingrained.

I had just decided to leave and was walking back to the centre when a man in a drab suit began a conversation. He was a small slim man with a narrow face and a watchful manner who wore his dark suit without a tie, in the ubiquitous style that made Iranian men look like dishevelled Mormons. His name was Arselan, he said, and he was a 'government worker' on his lunch break. He often came to the Poets' Monument to relax on the grass and enjoy the gardens.

'It makes us know our place.' He said, washing a hand over his beard. 'We are such a small part of everything, we must remember that always.' He thought for a moment, than continued with a smile. 'But what other country has fifty poets to bury together?'

Arselan seemed pleased with this and peeled off into a shop as we walked, emerging a moment later with a bag of pistachios. When I mentioned that the Poets' Monument had seemed impersonal, too modern to evoke Persian culture, Arselan said, 'Ah, then I will show you something different, something more personal. It is more personal because it is a person.' He laughed. 'Not a real person, a statue of Khaqani, one of our poets. He is buried at the mausoleum but his statue is here.' He gestured the way we were going.

The statue was in a square behind the Blue

Mosque, itself one of the city's main attractions. Khaqani was portrayed in classical fashion as a kind of Sinbad figure with turned up shoes and a gown and turban. The effect of this pleasingly life-sized monument was immediately comforting after the modernist edifice and the other cultural contradictions of the last few days.

Khaqani had been born in 1100 and had died in 1185 by the Western calendar. 'He was a travelling man also, like you,' Arselan told me.

Khaqani was a man in the mould of a true Persian poet. He had been raised by an uncle at the royal court in Azerbaijan, then under Persian influence, and educated in such staples as astronomy, history and theology – influences that would later surface in his writing. He wrote poetry from an early age and was for a time court poet before setting off on the Hajj. His tour of the Middle East led to some of his best known poems, while his spell in prison for abandoning the court led to his *Habsiyeh*, or 'Jail Ballad'. Khaqani wrote in a deliberately complex, stylised way and was one of the writers credited with helping Farsi retain its independence from Arabic.

Iran reserved a special place in its heart for literary figures like Khaqani. It is these men who have become household names today at the expense of

Arab figures better known elsewhere in the Muslim world. Poets like Omar Khayyam, Ferdowsi, Sa'adi, Hafez, and Rumi all influenced literature outside Iran as much as inside it. They were writing during the 11th–14th century Islamic high point, a kind of Renaissance without the Reformation, during which many of Islam made most of its important scientific and cultural innovations.

Some of the best known fictional Muslim characters too were Persian, appearing in stories like 'The 1001 Nights', first recorded during the 9th century. The framework of Sheherazade telling the stories to prolong her life was added sometime later in the 14th century to form the version we are familiar with today. It was the collection of stories present in Sheherazade that gave rise to Aladdin, Sinbad and Ali Baba, not to mention Sheherazade herself, entering the western consciousness during the 19th and 20th centuries thanks to the labours of Edward Fitzgerald and Edmund Dulac. Since then the stories have inspired operas, films and books.

I had thought that abstract monuments like the poet's tomb, and a couple of others I'd seen that looked like exhibits from a Seventies art gallery, were a response to the Muslim taboo against depicting people. It was another of the misconceptions I had bought with me into Iran. In fact the modernist fashion came much more from the Pahlavi dynasty's modernisation drive of the Sixties and Seventies, which peaked in the years before the revolution. The last Shah's megalomaniac streak had then added the element of scale and the result was this outlandish and irrelevant public architecture.

The modern Muslim taboo is more concerned with Muhammad only, a fact illustrated by the number of representations of Ali, the founder of the Shia sect, whose pictures were everywhere. In cafés, in shops, even inside cars, dangling from the mirror. It was a single sympathetic likeness repeated many times, showing a compassionate and humane man. A skilful portrait that gave him authority and saintliness with just the right amount of ethereal soft focus. Some-times – and when you became attuned to the pictures this was a huge difference – there was a bloody wound on his face. But I was to see this version later in Qom, the city of the Ayatollahs.

Iranians felt that their country was unique among the fifty or so Muslim countries around the world. When they explained this they tended to concentrate on aspects of their history other than Islam, which seemed strange at first. Of course theirs was also a Muslim history – undoubtedly all fifty of the dead poets were Muslim – but almost always the people I met preferred to concentrate on purely Persian historical events. When I tested people's feelings by asking if they were Iranian or Muslim, the answer was never Muslim. Sometimes people felt they were both, usually the older people (and in one of the world's youngest countries 'old' is anyone over 40) but most often the immediate response was: 'Iranian'. More than once the word came in an almost offended tone.

One young woman who came to sit at my table in a *chay* shop told me off for even asking. Islam was only the most recent part of their history, she said. All of that history made Iran the country it was today.

'We are not Arabs.' She shook her head emphatically. 'And we have not become Arabs since Islam came here. The languages are totally different for one thing. In English you say God and in Farsi we say *Khoda*, but in Arabic they say Allah.'

She cut at the air with her hand. 'It's totally different. And here Islam is part of society, *not* the other way around.'

It was something I was to experience again and again in conversation, especially with younger people.

The sentiment was interesting because it ran directly contrary to the Koran, which says that a

Muslim's primary identity must be just that: Muslim. This apparent rejection of the Koran's all-encompassing social programme was a surprise; almost as much as it was to hear the rejection spoken so readily. History to Iranians was the 2,500 years since the beginning of the Achaemenid period, and the people who spoke to me never forgot to make this point. Sometimes, as with the woman in the *chay* shop, it was almost the only thing they said. They sat beside me already talking, at pains to point out that most of their history was independent, that much of their culture and many of their customs were distinctly Persian, and their language separate.

That evening at my hotel when the other women went to dinner, Sharin and I sat in the lobby talking. She had suggested the lobby because it was cooler, but it was also a place where the two sexes could meet unchaperoned. When I mentioned this Sharin dismissed it. This kind of thing didn't apply to her, she said with a twinkle in her eye. She was too old and in any case she was practically an American citizen.

'But you've still put on your *chador*,' I pointed out playfully.

'It is polite to go along with the rules.' She replied, though it was obvious she was tired of doing so. In any case her mind was palpably on something else.

She had come to my room to suggest the lobby and it was obvious she wanted to talk.

There were very few acupuncturists in Iran, of whom Sharin was one of three women. Acupuncture was a field about which there was no religious opinion, she said. If the Koran could be seen to be commenting on something, it was favoured or not depending on what was said. Or rather, Sharin stressed, on the mullahs' opinions of what was said.

Sharin had been educated in Britain and France and had finished with a degree at an American university. After her degree she had settled into a comfortable lifestyle for some years, happy to be out of Iran because this was the time of the revolution. Whenever she had news from home it was not encouraging. *Hijab* had been made compulsory, the Ayatollahs had taken over and the country had become an Islamic Republic. This was in the period immediately after the Revolution, the period when Ayatollah Khomeini and the temporary Assembly of Experts altered the draft constitution. While Khomeini had been in exile it had been a more inclusive, less Islamic document, though still too restrictive for many. After the Revolution major changes were made, chief among them greater power for the mullahs, plus a complicated system of unelected clerical vetting of government.

Add to this the creation of an unelected Supreme Leader, a post for which no one but Khomeini was ever considered, and technically the country had changed beyond all recognition.

In the circumstances Sharin would not have chosen to return to Iran. Life was comfortable in America. She could wear what she wanted and talk to whom she pleased. She was happy living in the West, until the day she received a phone call. The nightmare phone call that everyone away from home dreads, telling her that her mother had died.

Sharin came back for the funeral, then stayed for a week with her father. During that week Sharin was appalled by what she saw in Tehran. There were *Pasdaran*, the 'Revolutionary Guard', on the streets telling people how to behave; the age at which women could marry had been lowered from eighteen to thirteen (nine with the father's permission); and Khomeini was saying things like 'there is no subject upon which Islam has not expressed its judgement'. He was turning the clock back, Sharin said, telling people not to expect democracy because it was a Western subversion. This was to be a purely Islamic state. Anyone interpreting the law, 'in a manner contrary to the divine will' was committing 'the sin of innovation'.

With her father living alone in such a country,

Sharin felt compelled to wind up her practice in America and move back to Iran. She went to live with him in north Tehran and became a teacher at the Tehran University medical faculty, a large and well respected department. Within a couple of years she had fallen in love with one of her students, despite the fact that he was much younger, married him and moved to a small flat of her own. A year later Sharin had started an acupuncture clinic in a leafy north Tehran suburb, and was gaining a reputation as a teacher. Her father too eventually remarried, a woman from the countryside Sharin had never met.

At some point – Sharin's memory was a little hazy – she had asked a lawyer friend to look after the family's legal papers and quite by chance he recognised her step-mother's name. The friend was intrigued and did some digging. To Sharin's horror he unearthed a previous marriage, unknown to Sharin's father but preserved in the marriage certificate.

Sharin was scathing in her opinion of her step-mother. In her telling, the woman was an uneducated trollop, an unscrupulous villager on the make, hands and feet rough, everything in between youthful and yielding, given over to successive husbands.

After agonising for months Sharin told her father what she knew, but she found him unwilling to listen.

He reminded Sharin that he had also been married before.

Years passed during which Sharin had a child of her own, a son; and in which Sharin saw less and less of her father. Then came the news one winter that her father too had died.

Sharin plucked at her *chador* and looked at the lobby carpet. Darkness had fallen in the street outside and through the hotel's glass doors the rear lights of cars pulsed along a road packed with evening shoppers. In the lobby fluorescent lights glared on the gilded mirrors and glass tabletops; a bulky air-conditioner wheezed in a corner.

All of which I noticed because Sharin was silent for so long I thought she wouldn't continue. The day was ending in a muggy crescendo and I dearly wanted a cold drink, but the bitterness with which Sharin had described her step-mother made it plain there was more.

Several years after her father died, when things had again settled down and her son was six, problems began to develop in Sharin's own marriage. Her husband became distant and preoccupied, and while it was true that he had been promoted, Sharin thought she recognised something else. Eventually she confronted him and he admitted what she already knew, that he was having an affair. She didn't want anything to change and so she did nothing, hoping her life could return to normal. But her husband had been galvanised by the forced admission and soon afterwards he moved out, taking their son.

Sharin was shattered, but still there was worse to come. Over the next few months it became obvious that her husband's affair hadn't finished, and that in fact it was with Sharin's step-mother. Her husband had come to know the woman during the breakdown in Sharin's relationship with her father, when he acted as a go-between, relaying messages and taking their son to visit. The long working days that had so distracted him had in fact been spent at the woman's flat in north Tehran; the flat that once belonged to Sharin's father.

Her husband sued for divorce and Sharin was granted one supervised visit with her son each week. As a matter of principle she refused this. He was her son too, she snorted, care should have been divided equally. To accept one day a week, and that with a sheriff present, was to accept a form of punishment from the court. Sharin had stuck to her guns too; her son was now nine and she hadn't seen him for two years.

6

Half the World

For the first five days after Tabriz the desert was unchanging in its uniformity. Sunrise and sunset were linked by the black ribbon of tarmac and by the routines that quickly became familiar and comfortable. The Alborz mountains kept pace to the left, shepherding the road south-east against a line of low hills to the right. I bought food in villages and small towns and stopped here and there at road houses for *chay*. I cooked each evening in the desert, balancing a single pot on the camping stove, boiling water, stirring pasta, eating whatever I'd found during the day in the way of raisins or bread. Then, as late as possible, I crawled into my boiling, airless tent and slept.

Being in the desert was like looking up from a book to focus on some distant object. Immediately the world was wide and bright again, and, with foreground detail and distraction removed, simpler and less demanding. The cares and concerns of the city drifted away and were replaced by a preoccupation with more basic necessities. Food, water, shelter and travelling became the wonderfully liberating objectives of each day. Success was measured only by progress through the landscape: recognising road signs, looking for food and water, sustaining energy, dealing with traffic, meeting people, beating the heat. To those who stay at home travel can sometimes seem like a gorgeous lethargy, yet for the traveller each day is a barrage of near-manic activity.

Coryate too must have been equally engaged by each day as he continued his walk through this inhospitable landscape. Among unfamiliar people with nothing but the few possessions he carried, he was constantly exposed to new dangers, either from the landscape itself or from the potential confusions of language and custom. Of the few Englishmen who had so far made it through Iran, only two had written accounts of their experiences. It is not certain that Coryate read either of these, or indeed that he had any other information that would have been of use to him. He was essentially making it up as he went, like any pioneer. To Coryate the only way to find out what was possible, was to do it. In the empirical spirit of the Enlightenment he was his own experiment.

Perhaps also the somewhat Puritan style he was

either brought up with, or adopted early, shows through here. He didn't wait to be shown the way, he didn't follow anyone's lead nor did he ally himself to one of the great men of the day. Advancement by connection was something that Coryate had turned his back on when he left England. There were no factions to join in the desert and no one to turn to for help. He had chosen to eschew the comfort of such allegiances by remaining an independent traveller. In one of the letters he even indirectly scolds himself for accepting the hospitality of English merchants in India '... and although a year is too long a time to spend in one place,' the place in question being the merchants' factory (warehouse) in Agra.

The lack of centralised control favoured by the Puritans, along with their wish to simplify, or 'purify', life might well have played a part in Coryate's sometimes pig-headed bravery. It probably also played a part in his decision to walk, and he certainly emphasised this means of travel whenever possible, virtually adopting it as his identity. To use only what God had given was meritorious, and to Coryate was a way of establishing a place for himself.

Possibly to protect the potential bonanza his journey from Tabriz to the Mughal frontier would later bring, his coverage of this section is again limited. He gives only a few comments and a sketchy itinerary, and these almost incidentally in one of the letters.

However disappointed I had been with Samuel Purchas' editing I would gladly have traded it for what I had now, which was essentially nothing. And knowing so little made me want to know everything; like a spoilt child I wanted what I couldn't have, simply because I couldn't have it. I wanted to know what Coryate saw, how he felt, what he ate, who he met. I wanted him to bring me the sights and smells of seventeenth century Persia. Instead all I had was 'from Gazvin I had 23 daies to Spahan [Esfahan]'. It was the only time when I was to feel let down by Coryate; the only time when this most verbose of men seemed to have too little to say.

∽

On the main Tabriz-Tehran highway, at a village near Zanjan that was all dusty alleys and orchards, I was invited to the home of a young man called Malik. We met in a ramshackle *chay* shop a little way from the highway and chatted about his studies. He was a student in Tehran and had come home for the weekend – Friday in Iran – to visit his parents. They and three generations of his family lived in a rambling old house in an apricot grove at the edge of the village. Malik's grandfather had come from Tehran in the mid-Sixties when Ayatollah Khomeini was exiled and I assumed he must have been a cleric of some sort. Since then the family had lived quietly as small-scale farmers and landowners.

Malik was now seen as the success of the family, because he was the only grandson and because he was studying computer sciences in Tehran. He would work in the capital when he graduated, he said as we trod on our shadows to the house. The kind of job he wanted, developing software for the Farsi market, was easier to find there, and of course better paid.

At dinner that evening we sat on wonderfully soft embroidered cushions and ate from dishes strewn on a tablecloth on the floor. Tabrizi carpets and rugs gave the feeling of turf while behind us various bolsters and cushions were piled against unadorned white walls. A large earthenware urn in a cast-iron frame in one corner completed this minimalist's fantasy of hospitality.

Malik sat beside me translating the polite small talk until he gently encouraged me to start eating, as no one else would begin until I had. With the meal underway the family then went off at a tangent among themselves while I made the most of the simple, delicious food. As I ate the smaller children ran around the back of the group and giggled at me, but I was too exhausted to play with them and Malik gently shooed them away.

He was nodding thoughtfully at the conversation and putting in the occasional word.

'It is about marriage,' he said, turning to me. 'My aunt was talking about it then. She lives in Tabriz, and before that in Tehran. Women are more Western in those cities, and of course in Tehran there are many outside influences. It is not like in the country where people are more religious. People in Tehran are religious as well, but in the country ...'

I suggested that they were more traditional and perhaps less well educated.

Malik dropped his eyes and nodded. He paused to take some chick peas with a piece of flat bread. 'She is educated,' he said, nodding towards his aunt, 'but my family is not. When I studied in Tabriz I lived in her house. Her opinion is that a woman must marry who she chooses, and that the marriage is invalid if a woman is forced to marry by her family. But my grandmother has said it is not true. It is for a family to decide who is a good match. She is saying that love is not a good thing because it can lead you to choose the wrong person. In this matter a family knows better because they are not involved. My grandmother says that my aunt only says what she does because she met her husband in Tehran and she is pleased with her marriage. Usually it works best the other way.'

The grandmother's lined face was cushioned in the thick swathes of her *chador*, held in place with tucks and folds. Her brown hands were the only other part of her body that was visible either directly or in shape, and they moved constantly, passing food to her plate, tearing the thin bread, scooping vegetables to her mouth.

'But have more food'. Malik said, smiling at me. I was cross-eyed with fatigue and the wonderful meal was almost too much.

'This is *fesanjan.*' he said, loading my plate. 'It is made with pomegranate and nuts, and some meat also. This one,' he fished around apologetically in the bowl, 'this one has some chicken.'

Fesanjan was delicious. It was one of a few Persian dishes I came across that mixed fruit with meat in a uniquely Iranian way. I found it everywhere, and with enough variation that each time was different.

∽

A range of low hills drew the road on and to the south, away from Gazvin and the influence of the Alborz mountains. At a place called Buni I spent a frustrating hour looking for the Qom road. My ancient map and Iran's population increase confused the issue so that what should have been a village was now a town, with the crossroads buried among new buildings. Eventually I went out of the centre to the east, directed by a man on a motorcycle who rode beside me to a junction. From here, he said, pointing at the desert, it was a straight road to Qom.

I camped that night in the middle of nowhere with only the heat and the dust for company, and came to Saveh the following day. When Marco Polo visited the city in the 13th century he found the tombs of the Magi here, the biblical 'three kings' who set out from 'the east' to visit Bethlehem. The men had been buried side by side in three sarcophagi and were, according to Polo, still whole with beards, hair and flesh all intact. Today the city is a scruffy and unremarkable place, all mud brick walls and small-scale urban disrepair. There was rubble in the side streets I cycled in and torn posters of politicians on lampposts and walls. The city had been important during the Achaemenid period before its fortunes waned. During the Safavid period its position on the trade routes made it important once again, until 1796 when the capital was moved to Tehran and Saveh found itself off the main trade route. Thereafter the city sank gently into provincial decline.

In town I was told, very proudly, and by a man, that Saveh's history had recently been eclipsed by the election of a female mayor. Parliamentary elections a few months previously had been mirrored by local elections and the woman, Mehri Roustaie Gherailou, had been returned with a big majority. She was unique, the man said happily, as the only female mayor in Iran.

I asked if Iran had used a mayoral system before the revolution and if there had been female politicians then, but the man wrinkled his nose dismissively. He was middle-aged and his full beard and neat collarless shirt hinted at a religious background. He was talking about Iran after the Revolution, he said, the recent period in which the theocracy had brought order and stability. He told me something of the notorious excesses of SAVAK, the last Shah's secret police, and then moved to the domestic peace Iran enjoyed today, skipping everything in between. The Revolution was still fresh in his mind and Saveh's female mayor was shining vindication of the theocracy.

His head bobbed earnestly. Yes, yes, he laughed, Iran had female politicians just like the West.

⌒

Mehrab yelled into his mobile phone as we drove through Qom. We were on our way across town to pick up a friend of his, a young man who was apparently a cleric and who could get us into the Shrine of Fatima. He had access to this most holy of places, in this most holy of cities, because his family had connections with the shrine. But when we met the man he was distant and I found Mehrab had exaggerated both his friendship and the man's connections.

Mehrab was round-faced with black hair and a boyish demeanour. He had the kind of face that would probably look seventeen for the rest of his life. He was eager to please and quick-witted enough to anticipate conversation, even in English. Some of the students and theologians in Qom had recently started learning English, he said, in order to get the Shia message to a wider audience. They were adopting the internet as a way of doing this and already some of the Ayatollahs, including Khameini, had their own websites, although most were in Farsi; one Ayatollah even had a blog.

'This is Ashkan,' Mehrab said, introducing the friend. 'He is studying in a seminary here but he doesn't speak English.'

Ashkan was tall and slim with hooded eyes and a

neat beard. He wore a black turban and the full clerical outfit that gave the streets of Qom such a dramatic
feel. He was softly-spoken and didn't say much in any
language. It quickly became obvious that Ashkan
had no intention of taking us on a guided tour. He
drew his brown cloak in defensively and folded his
arms. Mehrab switched to English after a few sen-
tences, launching into some praise for Ashkan as a tal-
ented young scholar. He seemed to be a leading light
somehow, although I had the idea that Mehrab knew
him better by reputation than in person. The man
simply looked over our heads and waited for Mehrab
to stop speaking.

He said a few unenthusiastic words in Farsi, then
without looking at me said goodbye in English.

'He has got to leave.' Mehrab said. 'He is teaching
a class this evening and he also has his own studies.
He will become a mullah. He is a good man.'

We walked past a car park full of pilgrim buses and
across the river to the shrine complex of Fatima. The
piazza was crowded with families constantly crossing
and recrossing, talking, smiling, taking photographs,
pointing to the stunning blue and gold domes and
the stout minarets. There was an air of excited confusion, as though they had just arrived at a fairground
and couldn't decide which ride to go on first. Mehrab

said he thought they looked like good people and apologised that I couldn't go into the shrine. It was for Muslims only, a tradition that had prevailed since the Safavid era.

The shrine had been rebuilt and expanded during that time to emphasise the emerging Shia identity of the Persian renaissance. Since then it had become increasingly popular with pilgrims to the point where it was now one of the holiest Shia sites.

The reverence for Fatima, daughter of the seventh Imam and sister of the eighth, illustrated one of the main differences between Sunni and Shia Islam. The Sunni held that when Muhammad died he had appointed no successor, in fact none were worthy to lead in the way he had. The Koran and the Sunnah themselves (including Muhammad's *Hadith*, the 'sayings of the prophet') were the authority. Social leadership could therefore come from elected or appointed political leaders who were separate from the clergy with the two systems running in parallel. The Shia, on the other hand, held that Muhammad had appointed Ali, his cousin and son-in-law, as successor and that Ali's descendants could rule as both political and religious leaders. The English word 'caliph' comes from the Arabic *khalif*, meaning successor or descendant, and expresses this concept of leadership; a concept that continues in modern Iran with Khomeini's creation of the position of Supreme Leader.

The Shia believe that after Muhammad there were twelve Imams, ending with Imam Muhammad al Mahdi, otherwise known as the *Mahdi*. The 'Twelvers' wait in a born-again Christian fashion for the appearance of their saviour. At that time all injustice will be swept away and the true believers will be rewarded.

Mehrab was keen for me to know these details and explained the basics as we walked to a nearby internet café. There was nothing sinister about Islam or about Shi'ism, he said. Everything was open and honest. To prove this we went and checked Mehrab's blog. It was very fashionable to have such a thing in Iran but still a general fear of the authorities made him use a public computer. Sometimes his blog got comments, he said, and you couldn't control what people wrote. Sometimes these comments were inflammatory or critical of the mullahs. His was one of the most popular blogs from Qom because he wrote about everyday life here. And because he knew some of the clerics and seminary students and wrote about them too. I became increasingly interested and began to imagine his blog as a kind of theocratic *Hello* magazine, although once we had logged on it turned out to be a rather sober Farsi page with just a few small photographs.

The Iranian love affair with the computer was already quite advanced by the time mass communication became electronic. The internet quickly became a place where the two sexes could meet without contravening any of the strict morality rules. And also a place where opinions could be expressed more freely, as long as certain precautions were taken. A survey had recently shown that the greatest number of people entering the word 'proxy' into search engines were Iranian. A proxy server meant that the end user was once removed from their blog or web search and made the authorities' job of tracking them harder. But track them they did, resulting in interrogations and arrests in a few cases for people who by demanding equal rights for women, for example, had 'disturbed the peace', or 'threatened the security of the nation'.

A woman could be rebellious from her own home using the internet, without risking a 'bad *hijab*' fine in the street. Iranian blogs, and there were many, all seemed to give some sort of political opinion as some point, ranging from direct and angry criticism to much lighter comment. One blogger, writing in English, chided herself for almost forgetting to wear her *chador* when leaving her flat, talking about it in the way a European might when forgetting an umbrella. Yet even so innocuous a comment could be seen as implicit criticism and draw censure.

As the only foreigner in the café I soon began to attract a crowd and a discussion developed about which blogs were the most representative. When I asked about blogs that expressed dissent Mehrab became visibly nervous and suggested we go home. It was late anyway and as usual I was exhausted so I didn't argue. We collected the car and drove back out of the centre to his family's flat in the suburbs. We ate another of the delicious meals I was constantly fed in Iran and I helped Mehrab with some questions he had about English. Then I went into the bedroom he had vacated for me and fell asleep wondering what the day's blog might contain.

〜

From Qom the road gradually climbed as it ran to the west around the Karkas mountains. My map showed villages of various sizes along the way, although some turned out to be figments of the mapmaker's imagination. Beside the road the desert was entirely sand in places, and dotted with tufts of vegetation like sponges on the sea floor.

In a couple of the villages I was invited in by

friendly families who served me banquet-sized meals that made it difficult to stay awake. They were effusive and caring, but once I had closed the door to sleep there was never a sound. Outside the villages I camped again, and even slept one night on the bonnet of an enormous articulated lorry I came across parked in the desert.

I found the driver in the shade under the truck, tinkering with something that looked as if it shouldn't be tinkered with. He mimed being impressed with the bike, then with a cheeky smile mimed that I should help him with something. He knew of a roadhouse a few miles away, he said, where I could get dinner. As there was no traffic and he couldn't hitch, would I ride there and get some food if he paid for it?

The prospect of a free dinner was too good to miss, so I took the message he wrote and bought the food back tied to the handlebar in a plastic bag. We ate in the truck's cab with the driver adding bread and cucumbers to the meal. Afterwards I brewed tea on the camping stove and we played Frisbee in the desert with my plate until it was dark.

The following night I slept in the desert beside the tent solely to watch the stars again. I had somehow missed them before that evening, but the night on the truck's bonnet had been a revelation. I was so amazed that I spent all of the next day anticipating that night, like a lover waiting for his sweetheart. There was something so wholesome about moving through the desert all day by your own effort, then sleeping unafraid beneath the heavens. There was a sense of communing with something that was heightened by the desert being potentially so hostile a place. The Milky Way was so clearly visible that its changing position in the sky kept good time and I found myself waking to check it like a schoolboy with a new watch.

～

In Esfahan I met a student by the name of Mahta outside my hotel when she asked if I would do her English homework for her. Mahta was difficult not to like because of this boldness; and because it was tempered with a polite, inquisitive spirit I couldn't refuse. She was taking extra English classes during the summer holidays and the task was to transcribe a recorded passage from the BBC World Service. She gave me a small tape recorder along with ten excruciatingly complex minutes of news: would I call her when it was done, she asked, and scribbled down a phone number. When I called she invited me to dinner with her family by way of thanks.

The following evening Mahta and her father came to collect me, both apologising at once, Mahta in English and her father in Farsi.

'What I want to say is sorry for being late,' Mahta said, 'but you know lateness is our national hobby.' She was smiling nervously so I assured her it wasn't a problem. Still a little nervous she went on talking, embarrassed at first but gaining confidence quickly.

'We want to build a house in the north-west of the city, but it is difficult. Our flat is only in the east of the city, so it is not so good.'

Iranians preferred the north-west of their cities because prevailing winds came from that direction, bringing fresh air from the desert. The least popular suburbs were in the south-east where the pollution accumulated.

We drove on through streets lined with trees and busy with people, turning many times into progressively smaller and quieter streets. Mahta talked about her friends, one of whom, Zohra, she had spent time with that afternoon. Part of what made Mahta so forthright was the pressure she and her friends felt at school. There were exams every year and each one played a part in her future. She simply had to do well, she said, and was unafraid to take what advantage she could. She had a year left to study and poor results now

146

would mean trouble later. She might not get into a good university, or worse still have to go to a paying university. Her family were not well off and she knew this would be hard for them, and besides, private universities were considered inferior to the state colleges.

The family flat was in a short, narrow street lined with parked cars and full of children. Once inside, the space opened out into an open plan kitchen-dining room, with a sofa opposite the TV in the lounge and a picture of the Ka'ba with a clockface on the wall above. Apart from that picture we could have been in any Western country.

As soon as we were inside, before even the door had closed, Mahta took off her *chador* and threw it into a corner.

'I hate wearing my uniform.' she said with a frown. 'Every day I must wear it – every time.'

There was a childish squeak from behind a door and a small black-haired boy exploded into the living room. Mahta introduced me to her younger brother, Reza. I shook hands with him and he showed me some karate kicks.

Mahta explained that her mother had recently stopped him doing martial arts, because she thought it was bad for his development, with the consequence that he ran around the flat non-stop.

We went to the table, which was covered with food, and Mahta's mother calmed Reza down enough to join us.

After a few general comments in Farsi, Mahta began speaking English and immediately the tone of what she was saying seemed to change. She had a kind of boyfriend, she said, who had lived in Esfahan until last year when his parents moved to Tehran. They had spoken a couple of times since then, although not recently. They were both feeling the pressure of their schoolwork and she thought they might not speak again. The boy was studying chemistry and was intelligent enough to do well, but he was also 'political', as Mahta put it. He had been involved in a demonstration at the Esfahan university the previous year. She knew some of the other people involved because they were older siblings of classmates, people she met socially, people from good families. Some of those students had been killed in the demonstration, she said, when the police moved in to break it up. Later news reports labelled the victims 'criminal elements'.

'But,' Mahta said leaning towards me, even in her own home, 'I knew those people. They were just students like me. What I want to say is that the government *lied*.'

Mahta stared at the table for a moment. It had

been a seminal moment in her young life, one that had perhaps changed things. She had already said her mother was quite devout, and that her father usually followed the government line because of his military career. That evening, as we sat talking in English, Mahta already seemed partly estranged from her parents. For their part, they had been silent for most of the meal, content to listen to their daughter speak in a language that was becoming the hallmark of the younger generation.

English was almost a refuge for Mahta. If she could become a doctor, as she hoped, she could change the temporary enchantment she had conjured by hosting a foreigner, into the reality of going abroad. But to be accepted to study medicine required the highest marks at school, in the exams she was soon to take. Mahta too fell silent. She toyed with some salad until her mother made a move to refill my glass and Mahta was prompted to become the hostess once more.

Much later, when it was time to leave, I said goodbye to the family, including the little brother who was still up and kicking, and Mahta and her father took me back into town. On the street outside my hotel Mahta shook my hand, even though it was illegal, and gave me her address in Farsi so that I could write.

'Ten years ago, when I came back to Iran, no one had this surgery', Rana said. 'People were afraid because they were laughed at, but now it has become fashionable. A quarter of the patients I see want this rhinoplasty.'

Rana spoke with an American accent and seemed to know so much about cosmetic surgery that I thought she was a surgeon.

'No, no,' she laughed in delight. 'A psychologist – I counsel these people.'

She said that most of the time they didn't need surgery because there was nothing wrong.

'They are doing it for vanity, or sometimes because of psychological problems. I treat the people who are obsessive about it.'

Rana had joined me on the grass quite spontaneously, despite being alone, and seemed unperturbed by the occasional stare we drew. People would assume we were married, she said with a grin, and as long as the police didn't check, we could talk.

We were sitting in Esfahan's vast Naqsh-e Jahan square, one of the largest squares in the world and the centrepiece of Shah Abbas' 17th-century capital. Around the periphery shops, cafés and even a post office drew a constant stream of people. A fountain the size of a tennis court was lost in the centre and everywhere families picnicked beside well-watered shrubs. At either end marble pillars that had once been the polo goalposts now stood forgotten. The square had originally been intended as a polo ground, to be viewed from the shady columned portico on the roof of the Ali Qapu palace to one side, although Abbas had been inspired by the grandeur to make more of it. For the remainder of his reign he beautified the square as the centre of his jewelled city. Today it is one of those unique places in the world which are equally appealing to locals and to visitors, and is constantly filled with both. It had since been called Shah square before the revolution, and was now called Imam square, although Rana encouraged me to call it Naqsh-e Jahan, the original name that meant something like 'picture of the world'.

Our conversation was drowned out for a moment by the jangling bells and shouted conversation of a passing buggy, and a moment later by two small boys trying to hitch a ride on the back in perfect Dickensian style. Friday in the square meant fun for all the family: picnics on the grass, meetings, and the main weekly service in the Imam mosque.

I was interested to know more about why such a handsome and youthful people should want cosmetic surgery.

'Oh, you know what people are like ...' Rana said.

Sometimes those she counselled had already had surgery and wanted more. Some who recognised an unhealthy obsession in themselves contacted her; at other times the surgeons – the good ones – referred people when they thought there might be a problem.

'I just talk to them,' Rana said, 'like in a discussion so they can understand and correct the problem – but you are educated, you know what a psychiatrist does.'

'You know the worst thing about many of these plastic surgery clinics is that the surgeons are not qualified. It is a big problem in Iran. I studied in the United States and got my qualifications there but not so many people can do that. We don't have good relations with other countries and so people study in Iran instead.'

The result was that doctors could change fields with relative ease, meaning surgery could be carried out by someone with little specific training. There were many clinics in Esfahan and only a few were properly registered or accredited.

'Sometimes people pay just a hundred dollars for an operation, but the doctors are not good so then people must find a specialist to fix the problem. Sometimes this surgery ruins people's lives, that is why I am against it.'

She propped herself on her arms, hands in the cool grass.

'But this surgery will always be popular here', she went on, 'because women must hide their bodies. Only their faces can show, so it natural to make the best of them. And hands too. Did you know we have plastic surgery for hands?'

Every day in Esfahan I saw half-a-dozen altered faces. White plaster splints covering noses; black eyes from eye-lid surgery; swollen mouths from cheek reduction; puffy jaws from god knows what. And these mugging victims wore their trauma with pride. It confirmed their membership of an elite group. It was even rumoured in Esfahan that Tehranis, their rich and vacuous cousins, sometimes wore a nose splint without having had the surgery.

The political system that forced women to wear the *chador* and so bought about the cult of the face, a political system that was almost exclusively male, had become its own victim. The Nose Job was so irresistible that not only did the mullahs' daughters have them, but men too fell victim. At first I thought these splints were sporting injuries – Iranian men are almost clinically obsessed with football – but after talking with Rana it seemed that these faces too were the product of titivation. Iranian women were leading their men in this subtle way, telling them how to feel and behave.

When Rana left I went into the Ali Qapu palace behind where we had been sitting. Of the three buildings in the square this was the simplest and most elegant, although the other two, the Imam mosque and the Sheikh Lotfollah mosque were more splendid.

The palace structure was intact and although the interior was bare and needed renovating, there was still some decoration. Much to my delight this included two small, unlabelled frescos of a man and woman, rubbed away almost to nothing. They were just recognisable as Jacobean, and both were in western clothing. For a moment I couldn't stop myself thinking that the man might be Coryate, although the date of the original decoration predated his visit to Iran. And the portrait just didn't look like Coryate either. The man was dressed too conventionally as a Puritan, and bore no resemblance to the engraving in the *Crudities*. In any case it seemed that Coryate passed through without a trace, as I had already realised. The concept of him sitting for a portrait and not repeating the story in one of the letters was unthinkable for such a shameless self publicist.

The portraits must have been of Robert Sherley and his Armenian bride, known to Shah Abbas, and from exactly the right period. Both were portrayed here in European dress, no doubt to add to the exotic spectacle of the palace. Despite the years of damage I was sure it could only be Sherley. I felt this was confirmed, if a little obliquely, by a tour guide who I managed to speak to briefly as she marshalled a group of tourists around the building. The portraits were of an Armenian noble couple, she said, and although she didn't know their names she agreed they were probably the original decoration.

7

The Desert Prophet

'Muslims don't eat pork,' Hamid was saying, 'that's true, but we are not Muslims, we are atheists.'

'You're ... an atheist?' I spluttered.

'Oh, yes,' he went on. 'I am definitely an atheist, and I think he is too.' He jerked a thumb at Sharif, who agreed he was. The three of us were walking through Chehel Sotun Palace, another of Esfahan's well preserved palaces and one of the most attractive Safavid buildings anywhere, after I had bumped into the pair the previous evening. Chehel Sotun was relatively small with a cosy feel and set in a park of mature trees. To the front an oblong pool bordered by flower beds stood before a wide portico which looked a little like a theatrical stage. Tall timber columns supported a high, elegant roof the entire height of the three-storey building, with state rooms leading from the stage on either side through ornate doors.

We had come into one of the main rooms and were standing below a series of colourful and detailed murals showing scenes from Safavid court life. Shah Abbas defeating The Turk, Abbas enjoying domestic life, Abbas receiving foreign dignitaries in his new capital. Each painting was set into a shallow blind arch separated by intricately decorated buttresses that lead up to vaults decorated with floral arabesques and intricate geometric patterns. The effect of such sumptuous decoration was slightly undermined by the lack of furniture or the other accoutrements of daily living.

Coryate had spent two months in Esfahan, then as now an enlightened and intellectual place. He was waiting here for a change of caravan to take him further east on the last leg of his journey and no doubt he used the time to see what he could of the city. I wondered if he had managed to talk his way in here, although as the palace was in use at the time, it was doubtful. But just for fun I imagined him holding forth to a bemused Shah, regaling him with the tale of his European travels and his unique book.

I was brought back to the conversation by Hamid's voice at my side. 'Religion is what is wrong with our country Danny, that's why we hate it.'

It was already clear that Iran's youth was heading rapidly away from the previous generation, yet such

158

a confident assertion was unexpected. Religion was a matter for the individual, he said, not the state. He repeated this with such vehemence that I asked if he had any sympathy for Islam at all, even as part of Iranian culture?

'Tradition is fine,' he said, 'I don't mind that. We have many traditions here but religion should stay there, in the past, not rule our lives now. The mullahs are a big problem in this country. They are corrupt, they live in big houses, they are arrogant and they have too much power.'

I had no real idea if what Hamid was saying was true, but just the fact that he said it was significant. The dichotomy between the younger generation and those in power was steadily increasing, leaving more and more people feeling disenfranchised. The parliamentary elections a couple of months before my visit had effectively been rigged by the theocratic element of the government. The Guardian Council, an unelected twelve-member body with the ability to veto any law and much else besides, had barred thousands of candidates from standing, the great majority of whom were reformers. Hamid's blanket dismissal of the clergy as corrupt showed how low public respect for them had sunk since the Revolution.

We ambled a little way carried along by the crowd

as it dawdled from room to room. One of the paintings showed the Shah in battle on a conspicuously white elephant; another portrayed a risqué court scene that included gay and lesbian couples and a dancing girl in a see-through top. They were all portraits from exactly Coryate's period, showing the clothing and perhaps even the behaviour Coryate had encountered and I wondered what he would have thought of that dancing girl. The *Crudities* had portrayed him as something of a prude on seeing Margarita Emeliana, the famous bare-breasted courtesan in Venice, though not enough to actually stop him asking for an interview.

I commented on the murals and on how these quite licentious images seemed to go against the often overbearing attitudes of the clergy and government. Why were these images not considered morally corrupting?

'These old men don't dare go against our history.' Hamid said with a wry smile. Then, nodding at the paintings, 'They know they can only control our lives now, not how they were then.'

Like Hamid and Sharif more than half of Iran's population had been born since 1980. If the date is pushed back to 1975 the figure rises to 75 per cent, making three-quarters of Iran's population less than 30 years old. Iran had the mother of all generation gaps. And like their parents, who grew up under the Shah, the younger generation had also been brought up within strict and often harshly imposed limits. These twenty-something's now had chips on their shoulders too, just as their parents had before the Revolution.

'We are a time bomb.' Hamid said. 'We are finishing our educations and getting our first jobs. In ten years we will be managers. Some of us will be politicians and have power, then there will be change. This is why I don't worry about politics. I don't like the mullahs, but they won't always be a threat, we must remember that. Their time is limited – Khameini is 67, and the other Ayatollahs are old men already.'

'And one is an old woman,' put in Sharif. 'There is one woman Ayatollah now – she is, *ahn*, butt-ugly.'

Sharif had a nasal twang to his speech which added to his innate comedy. A little later he pointed out a man in clerical clothes and said: 'That man is an Ayatollah, you can tell because he has the, *ahn*, tyre on his head.' I said the word was pronounced 'turban' but Sharif just laughed.

'These mullahs can't last forever.' Hamid went on. 'There are others to replace them, but gradually these people will come from my generation and they will be less intolerant. Things will change.'

Hamid talked about the career he would have as an engineer and about the rise of computers in Iran. He and Sharif wanted to be games programmers for the emerging software industry and were working on a game of their own, although work, study and other commitments were getting in the way. Sharif taught computing at summer school, and although Hamid was studying engineering, he was as proficient a programmer as Sharif: They felt they could do something in this new industry.

We walked through a set of decorated rooms that were being used as a museum, the odd glass case or display object bathed in coloured light from the stained glass windows.

Sharif talked about the graphics package they used in their programming, which was apparently the same programme used in Hollywood to make movies.

'It is called Maya.' He said. 'In America it costs $10,000 but in Iran I paid, *ahn*, $2.'

Hamid put in, 'Iran has no copyright agreements with any country, so we can get this software cheaply. And also DVDs, music, books – would you like some DVDs?'

I thanked him but said I couldn't carry them.

'It's one of the advantages of living in Iran.' He said. 'Some countries don't trade with us, but we can have any electronic media for free. We don't care about these trade restrictions, they don't hurt us because we trade with many other countries and already there has been too much American interference.' He smiled mischievously and said that Britain had been part of the problem too.

As the dominant force in the region after the First World War, Britain established Iran as a protectorate, mainly because of her oil reserves. This lasted just two years however, until Reza Khan, an army officer from one of Iran's Cossack brigades, seized power in 1921. His modernising, but somewhat anti-western, rule continued until the Second World War when Iran again tried to remain neutral. Initially this worked, until Hitler's invasion of the Soviet Union meant the Allies needed a supply route into Soviet territory. To gain this they invaded Iran, effectively ousting Reza Shah and installing his son who took the name Reza Shah Pahlavi.

With the war over the Shah allowed democratic elections to be held in which Muhammad Mossadegh was elected prime minister. To the horror of the West, and the delight of Iranians, Mossadegh set about nationalising the oilfields, a move so popular that its anniversary has since become a national holiday. The US response came courtesy of the CIA's dirty tricks department, which with British help backed a coup that overthrew Mossadegh in 1953. As part of the background noise of outside meddling, this coup also helped pave the way for the Islamic revolution twenty years later.

'We call the British "wily foxes", Hamid said. 'In Iran we remember the British Empire – India, Russia, the Great Game, it was all very … English.' He stuck out his chin in imitation.

'We are sure that Britain is still the mastermind in international politics,' Hamid said, 'making plans behind the scenes, controlling the US, pulling the strings in Iraq. Is that true Danny?'

I said that he should probably think more in terms of puppy than puppeteer.

'Ah, you disappoint me. We like the British here. We like to think British things are best. You know we have your cars here, we bought them in the Seventies.'

I thought he meant the Land Rovers I'd seen here and there, ancient pre-revolutionary things bucketing through the deserts or crawling through Esfahan's murderous traffic.

'No, no,' Hamid said, 'those are *good* cars, I mean the Peykans. You know, the identical cars you see everywhere, the noisy white ones.'

'They are always, *ahn*, smoking.' said Sharif. 'They

are Hillman Hunter, but we call them Peykan. It means arrow, for speed, but the cars are so old it is a joke. Like, *ahn*, bow and arrow technology. When they were no good in Britain, they came here. We bought the factory and everything and now we make them. Iran is, *ahn*, like a trash can.'

We were standing at the gate ready to go back out into the street when Robert, a friend of Sharif's, came by. After a couple of minutes of chatting everyone seemed reluctant to part so I suggested that we meet again the following day. There was a short discussion and Hamid asked, 'Would you like to see a synagogue? He is Jewish,' nodding to Robert, 'he could take us to see it?

‿

Jaqob Mollah Mari, or Mullah Jacob as he was sometimes called, was the spiritual head of the Jewish community in Esfahan in the late 18th century. Under him the community was thriving, as it had for many centuries. Unfortunately this success gave rise to jealousy among the city's Muslim leaders, who demanded Jaqob submit to a test to demonstrate which was the greater religion, Islam or Judaism. The task was nothing less than damming the Zayandah river itself, the main river through the city that watered its gardens and nourished its fields. A monumental challenge, but one that didn't worry Jaqob because, as he said, it would not be him who completed the task but God. Jaqob went to the Si-O-Sey Bridge, an elegant structure of thirty-six arches and one of the city's main tourist attractions now. He dropped a single pebble into the water, and to the horror of the mullahs the river was dammed. Angered by this miraculous proof the mullahs had Jaqob murdered and a pogrom was launched against the city's Jewish population.

Jaqob had been buried at a synagogue in the centre of Esfahan which was now dedicated to him, in a colourful sarcophagus decorated with blue and white Persian tiles. Since then, Robert said, the Jewish community had never fully regained its previous stature.

An hour previously we had walked the short distance from Sharif's flat to the building, which was completely hidden by a twelve-foot wall. Sharif had lived a couple of streets away for years, and had passed the building many times, but had no idea what was behind that wall. Even in the small courtyard it was not immediately obvious what the building was. Only inside the synagogue were there any signs of religion and these were far from ostentatious.

Apart from two small paintings, the order of

service and a list of previous Rabbis, the white wood-panelled walls were bare. The ceiling was low and white and a couple of strip lights filled the room with something like a medical glare. I recognised the same slightly apologetic shabbiness from the church in Tabriz. The synagogue had the same air of unobtrusiveness the Chaldean Catholics had adopted as their solution to life in the Islamic republic.

The pulpit (*bimah* in Hebrew) stood in the centre of the room surrounded by several rows of chairs in cheerful disarray. There was an area of colourful rugs and carpets to one side and several desks against one wall. The room looked like a recently abandoned classroom, and Robert told us that this was more or less what it was. Religious education was officially allowed within the three recognised religions of Iran, he said, Christianity, Judaism and Zoroastrianism, and children came here regularly to study.

'Officially Jewish children are allowed to miss some Islamic studies and come here,' he told me, through Hamid's translation, 'but they must also study Islam because for university entrance knowledge of Islam is required.'

Robert was a slim quiet man with dark hair in loose curls. He had a narrow jaw and looked vaguely Ethiopian. He was a little guarded in his manner and gave everything he said a great deal of thought; neither did he always answer questions directly. When I asked if he was happy with the government he told me about the Jewish member of the *majlis* – parliament – rather than giving his own opinion. All three of the acceptable religions had representatives in the *majlis*, although they were limited in their duties, being unable to elect other members, for example. Robert thought one member was about right for the 30,000 Jews in Iran, and that the 3,000 who lived in Esfahan suffered little overt persecution. When the odd synagogue window was broken it was usually petty vandalism rather than anti-Semitism.

Although Robert didn't say this, Hamid went on to add that a greater problem was with the sometimes sneering attitude of the local authorities. Since the Revolution the street beside the synagogue had been renamed Felestin (Palestine) street and the neighbouring square *Maidan-e Felestin*. Hamid nodded to himself. 'I should have known this was a synagogue when the street name was changed.'

Robert's uncritical view of the government was part of a pattern that was becoming more and more obvious. Especially when the placid, uncritical, Jewish Robert was being translated by Hamid and

Sharif. His assertion that everything was fine was too much to believe when Muslims – in this Islamic republic – had so much to complain about. If Muslims felt the system to be unfair because of its theocratic base, its restrictive laws, even its crappy old cars, surely it couldn't be the equitable place Robert was describing.

Robert wanted to show us the Torah and so we gathered around a cupboard in one corner of the room. He folded back the doors to show the scrolls, wrapped in embroidered cloth with two decorated finials protruding. I was about to ask if we could see the text when Robert got cold feet and closed the doors. We had reached the limit of his polite tolerance.

As with the Torah much of the building was modern, although the site itself was much older. There had been Jewish communities in Iran since the time of Cyrus the Great in the 5th century BCE; it was Cyrus after all who conquered the Babylonian empire and released its slaves, a great deal of whom were Jews. With his empire at its zenith, stretching from Afghanistan to Greece, Cyrus issued a proclamation that was effectively the first declaration of human rights. Recorded on a stone cylinder, which acted as a stamp, Cyrus gave citizens the right to worship freely, among many other things, or even to be atheists, and perhaps most significantly promised punishment for any official who didn't deliver.

Given such aspirational rhetoric many of the freed Babylonian Jews opted to move east and settle in Persia. The majority chose Esfahan, and once settled they quickly became successful merchants and Silk Road traders. So much so that by the Safavid period, 2,000 years later, Yuhudieh, Esfahan's Jewish quarter, was said to be larger than the Muslim quarter.

'We don't have so many problems,' Robert was saying, 'because most people in Iran don't associate us with Israel.' There was a slight pause as he stumbled over 'Israel'. 'The Zionist Regime' was the usual title, also used in Syria (and in Hamid's translation), but it probably wasn't a word Robert got to use very often.

'In Iran we know there is a difference between what a person thinks and what their government says. People here don't think all Jews are Zionists. That's very important.'

Jews in Iran were also helped by a *fatwa*, a ruling, from Ayatollah Khomeini promoting tolerance of religious minorities (with the exception of the Baha'i), although despite the *fatwa* Iranian law was still a long way from fair. Minorities were barred from the higher levels of government and were often subject to prejudicial treatment in civil courts. A Jewish person killed in an accident could receive only 20 per cent of the compensation a Muslim would receive, with the same ratio applying even if the death was murder. Other equally medieval laws said that the testimony of a non-Muslim counted for less than that of a Muslim, although this kind of prejudice was not restricted to religion because a similar law applied to the testimony of women.

Robert's rather sanitised version of Jewish life seemed to have come from the prevailing social conditions. Acceptance was one way people coped with this imbalance. They kept themselves out of trouble and insisted they were OK. Islam wasn't a problem for them, and they weren't a problem for Islam.

Robert's story of Mullah Jaqob reflected this by ascribing the emotion of jealousy to his murderers. Motives which shifted the blame away from religion and onto the personal failings of the men in question. It was the age-old adage: religions weren't bad, it was people who made bad use of them.

↪

Esfahan was one of the few places on Coryate's route that had a Christian quarter, and a large one at that. In the 17th century the city was laid out with the Muslim and Jewish quarters north of the river, and the Christian quarter of New Jolfa, to the south. A wide avenue of trees – now called Chahr Bagh, 'Four Gardens' – lead south to Si-O-Say Bridge. And across the river the avenue led through two miles of desert to Jolfa and Hezar Jarib, a large set of formal gardens to the south.

I followed the modern road south across the bridge along blinding streets and burning pavements. It was here in Jolfa that the Armenian Christians settled after Abbas' victory against the Ottoman Empire. They were given large areas of land south of the river, where something like two-dozen churches were eventually built, half of which remain today.

Vank Cathedral, the largest and most prestigious of these buildings, was buried among sleepy sun-struck streets. From the outside the cathedral looked a little like a mosque, with blind arches and other brick detailing below a very Persian dome. The building was perhaps five or six storeys high, although the square proportions made it seem smaller. Next to the building was a separate belfry in a more modern style with several graves below. But, as I discovered, the real interest was not outside the building at all, it was inside.

Every inch of the walls, from waist-height upwards, were entirely covered with a series of gorgeous 350-year-old paintings that was to be one of the greatest surprises in Iran; a kind of visual counterpart to the surprise of discovering atheists. Even window frames, doors and arches were elaborately decorated with angelic faces, floral designs and geometric patterns. I stood in the middle of the open floor wonderstruck by this hallucination, turning slowly beneath the gorgeous dome. The desert country outside of browns and greys was forgotten; the dusty roads, the parched landscape, the grimy cities. All were suddenly banished by the majesty of these clear, saturated, colours.

Alfred, an open-faced man in his twenties, saw me staring and asked if I had been to the cathedral before. He came here often because friends of his were connected with the church; he was amused at the concept of seeing it for the first time. He looked at me happily, recapturing some of this lost wonder as we craned our necks at the gorgeous gold and sky-blue tiles.

'Vank is like our Sistine,' Alfred said. 'It was also painted during the Renaissance. Well, during the late Renaissance.' Alfred's parents had sent him to be educated in a mission school in Bangladesh because it was the only way for an Iranian to get a good Christian education. He wanted to go into the priesthood in Iran and had used some of his time in Bangladesh to begin an informal study along these lines.

'I could not join a seminary there because I wanted to come home soon after finishing school. That was five years ago and still it is difficult to complete my training here. You are not free if you want to become a priest; the government makes problems for you, but I will finish my training.' He was confident of this, saying it in a way that sounded like a challenge.

We fell into a companionable silence for a few moments before he spoke again.

He pointed to a section of scaffold against one wall. 'You know all the restorers had to do was wash the walls. Inch by inch and very carefully of course, but that's really all they did.'

In 1664 a Venetian painter had been bought to Esfahan to decorate the interior, and he had made short work of the job, finishing it in months rather than the years then usual in Europe. He had painted onto dry plaster too, rather than using the tempera method, making the paintings more hard-wearing and the restoration much simpler. It had been a resounding success, judging by the luminous intensity of the paintings.

'The work should have been finished long ago,' said Alfred, 'but there is just one man and he works very slowly. He is not a Christian so I don't think he really cares.'

There was a surprising hint of dissatisfaction in this and so I asked generally about the church's dealings with the wider Muslim community.

Alfred shook his head emphatically. He said that things were difficult and that the problems were almost always with the government, who made it hard for them to live and work freely as practising Christians. He added that he thought the government was trying to acquire Christian land and mentioned a large cemetery about a mile away that had been given to them by Abbas, but which was now under threat.

Like every Iranian city Esfahan was expanding fast and this land, given freely 400 years ago, was now in a prime location. Alfred told me how patients in the neighbouring hospital were now complaining at the site of a graveyard from their windows.

He raised his eyebrows. 'But they knew it was there when they built the hospital. And by the way that is the worst hospital in town. It has such a bad reputation that sometimes people refuse to go there.' He gave a snort. 'They are thinking of closing that hospital, but in the meantime the cemetery is under threat. Do you see how it would work? The hospital would close, the government would take that land back, then try to get the cemetery as well. And you know what's next to the cemetery, the real reason they're doing it? A military base. The government is desperate to get its hands on that land.' He straightened his back. 'But our history prevents it.'

'We don't give them any trouble so they have no excuse to do anything against us. You know there is a meeting every month between the members of the cathedral board and the Ministry of Culture, as there is with all the religions. There are some presents given at these meetings.' He put his thumb on a crooked forefinger to show an envelope being passed over. 'It is how we stay independent. Of course we don't want to do this. The church is honourable, but everyone must pay this type of bribe in Iran.'

The museum of Armenian heritage next door was managed by a Christian, Alfred said. If they didn't, as a community, stay in the authorities' good books, the Ministry of Culture could replace him with a Muslim. It was within the law to do that despite the museum being a private institution.

At that moment Alfred's friends arrived. Two fashionable young couples, the women in colourful *manteaux* and the men in jeans, colourless shirts and sunglasses. Alfred asked if I would join them but it was already late in the day and I was leaving the following morning. I needed the evening to pack and prepare for the desert.

In the desert city of Yazd I met Daryush at the city's main fire temple. He worked on the long distance buses that thundered the hot tarmac each day between Yazd and Tehran, helping people with their luggage or with their needs during the journey. It was a ten-hour trip, he said, and there was always something to do. Once he had had to lift an entire car engine into the coach's luggage compartment — it was strange what people travelled with sometimes. Most of the time he just talked to people. Daryush now worked on the luxury coaches, called 'Volvo class', which served drinks and had air-conditioning. There were plenty of buses each day so he was never short of work.

Sometimes he met Zoroastrians on these buses, going to the fire temples or the towers of silence in Yazd or to visit relatives in Tehran. Daryush too was Zoroastrian, he said, although his name, the modern version of Darius, had already given this away.

Yazd was held to be the birthplace of Zarathus-tra, Daryush said, the religion's prophet and founder, although in truth no one really knew where he was born, or even exactly when. Linguistic evidence dated the *Gathas*, a series of hymns said to have been composed by Zarathustra, to around 1000 BCE, although there was little corroboration. The Avesta, which was sometimes called the Zoroastrian bible, wasn't compiled until the 4th century.

Yazd had been a city for 3,000 years and had always been a centre of Zoroastrianism, even as successive waves of conquest swept through the Persian heartland. Yazd was just far enough away from everything that it had been left to its own devices. When Islam did come, the city remained a Zoroastrian centre for many centuries afterwards. Today the numbers have dwindled to about 5,000 out of a population of half a million.

The fire temple was one of the largest in Iran, and one of the best known. It housed an Atash Bahram fire, the fire of victory and of kings, the most sacred and important of the three types of flame. This one, burning for 1,500 years, was easily the oldest. Tehran had most of the country's Zoroastrians, Daryush said, perhaps 15,000, with another 20,000 scattered around the country, but the temple at Yazd was the religion's spiritual home.

That was what bought people here, and that was how Daryush had met his wife. She was on one of his coaches, travelling with her parents on a family visit to the temple. Their courting had been easy, Daryush said. Certainly easier than it would have been for a Muslim couple. He had simply asked to see her again on the bus and they had kept in touch. Usually a man could never speak to a woman with her parents there.

Daryush's wife beamed a happy smile from his side. She also spoke some English, Daryush said, but she was shy. He laughed as she edged a little closer to him. She was like a child, her wide beautiful eyes shining from behind her husband's shoulder. They had been married for four years, Daryush said, although it seemed like four weeks. They came to the fire temple every so often although they did not think of themselves as religious.

Zoroastrianism had been called the first monotheism although it was often thought of as a dualism. Daryush smiled at this image of Ahura Mazda and his opposite number Angra Mainyu, gods of good and evil respectively, forming a half-way house between the many gods and the one.

'Some people say it started in India,' he said, waving a hand vaguely to show time and distance.

As the religion made its own journey from east to west the two approaches, the polytheism of ancient India and the monotheism of the Middle East, were linked not only through Zoroastrian but also an offshoot called Mithraism, a religion that may also have originated in Persia as much as 3,000 years ago.

The beliefs of Mithraism were laid down some time between then and around 400 BCE, although the religion is best known in a later, simpler, version, as the cult of Mithras, followed by Roman soldiers between 100 BCE and 400 CE. Various legends account for Mithras' birth, one of which has him as the offspring of Ahura Mazda and a virgin mother, with a birthday on 25 December: the 'Birthday of the Unconquered Sun'. He was born in a stable attended by shepherds, the stories say, and at the end of his life he ascended to heaven after sharing a last meal with his followers.

These similarities with Christianity are however not the coincidences they might seem to be. During the first centuries of Christianity it was decided, at places like the first ecumenical council in Nicea in 325 CE, that Jesus' birthday would be 25 December because it was already the mid-winter festival, and Mithras' birthday, and so would require less of a change in behaviour. Christianity went on quite shamelessly borrowing existing Mithraist practices, like the use of Sunday as the holy day, the symbolic use of bread, wine, and the cross, and appointing a 'pater', based in Rome, to head the religion. It was perhaps no surprise that once the Roman Empire had adopted Christianity, Mithraism was quickly stamped out.

Daryush and his wife showed me around the temple, which was so small as not to require it but they were keen that I missed nothing.

The building was a simple oblong with a portico across the front and a pool in the courtyard. Up a few steps into the building the *kalak*, the brazier holding the eternal flame, was in a separate room behind glass. On the walls in the main room there were holy texts and a picture of Zoroaster with a constant stream of people filing past both these and the window over-looking the flame.

'Most of these people are Muslim tourists,' Daryush said. 'They come on holiday to Yazd and to visit the temple. These are the open-minded people, the ones who are interested in Iranian history. The others don't come here: they don't even know where it is.'

Like the churches the temple was a low key build-ing. If you passed it in the street it was obvious, but from anywhere else in town it was invisible. There were no domes or minarets, no signs and no call to prayer. And the building also lacked any exterior decoration. There were none of the brightly coloured tiles or masonry details that made Iranian mosques so vibrant. The only adornment to the temple's simplic-ity was a crest in the centre above the entrance, Zoro-aster in an attitude of prayer between the outstretched

181

wings of an eagle, holding a disc, the same universal symbol I had already seen in Syria.

⌣

Kerman, a week to the south-east, was where things changed. The city was less a desert city than Yazd because it seemed less in tune with the environment; less part of the desert and more just in it. The centre of town was full of Seventies low-rise buildings and was all corners and anonymous glass.

In Kerman the people too began to change. It was here that I saw the first Pakistani men, recognisable by their faintly ridiculous *shalwar kameez* outfits like night-shirts with hopelessly baggy trousers. There were also noticeably fewer women in the streets, and those that I did see were dressed in the standard head-to-toe black.

At what was called the National Library of Kerman a charming white-haired man fussed over me for twenty minutes as I explained what I was looking for. He wanted a full explanation of Thomas Coryate and followed it with interest, even making some notes as I went. When I had finished he told me, without checking anything, that the only relevant material was an account of Anthony and Robert Sherley, contained in a Farsi history book.

Again there was nothing to do but leave, so I went to sit in the shade of a pomegranate tree outside. I was admiring the library's architecture, a mix of functional Persian mud bricks and classical columns, when the man came out holding a piece of paper with an address. Did I know there was a church in the centre of town, he asked? It was no longer functioning but it might be interesting for me to see it.

The church was a simple Islamic style box in Dr Shariati Street, Kerman's main thoroughfare. The manager of the taxi firm that now used the building's courtyard said it had been a florist's immediately after the revolution, and that Kerman's Christians had either moved to Esfahan or emigrated. Since 1979 the building had been left to slowly disintegrate; now the only people it attracted were vandals.

The church was made up of four plain rooms in a row across the back of the courtyard with three steps up at the front. Each room was full of builders' rubble, trash and human excrement. From the street outside the only clue to the building's history was a small sky-blue cross on either side of the entrance.

The manager of the taxi firm said there was another church in a nearby side street but that it was in worse condition. It seemed to me that anything any more ruined than what I was looking at, probably wasn't worth seeing, and as it was now late in the day I walked back to my hotel. It was not going to be the last time I gave up chasing a 400-year-old shadow around an unfamiliar city thousands of miles from home. In any case I had something else to do, a decision to make that I had been putting off for some time. Kerman was the last place I could make it, although I had the feeling I already knew the answer and it was not the answer I wanted.

Despite heat stroke and hitching a lift in Turkey, my trip in Coryate's footsteps had seemed a reasonable success so far. I had managed to follow his route quite closely and gained no end of insight into the hardships he had faced. Now there was something else to consider. The trip's major obstacle. The months it had taken to get here had not lessened the problem, as I had hoped it might by some miracle.

Dusk approached as I walked through Kerman's quiet side streets. The wind dropped and the air filled with the shrill cry of swallows sweeping backwards and forwards against the dusty orange sunset. In my room I closed the curtains, switched on the light and unfolded the map.

Part III

INDIA, PAKISTAN AND THE MUGHAL EMPIRE

Much of what we think of today as typically oriental comes from India, and much of that from the Mughal era. Indeed India's Muslim heritage, which eventually led to the partition of the country and the creation of Pakistan, is almost all Mughal.

Some of India's most memorable and characteristic architecture dates from this period. The Taj Mahal (though it post-dates Coryate), Delhi's Red Fort, Agra's fort, Fethpur Sikri and Srinagar's Shalamar Gardens are all Mughal, And while Lutyens' New Delhi dates from the early 20th century it is very much in the Mughal style.

What we think of as Indian food developed during this period when richly-spiced sauces were introduced from Persia. Also from Persia came artistic traditions such as painting, in which the Mughal artists excelled. When Sir Thomas Roe, the first English ambassador to India, gave Jahangir a portrait, his court artists copied it so well that Roe was hard put to tell the difference.

The dynasty began in 1526 with Babur, a descendant of the Mongol Timur (Tamerlane), although it was not until Akbar (r. 1556–1605) that it really took shape. Akbar encouraged the conflation of Persian and Indian artistic styles that became so distinctive, as well as promoting the continued progress in architecture. He was a tolerant man by the standards of the day and promoted complete religious freedom.

Jahangir and Shah Jahan, his son and grandson, continued most of what Akbar had begun though with progressively less religious tolerance. At the beginning of the 18th century, the dynasty began to fragment under the overly ambitious Aurangzeb. Thereafter the Mughal Empire lost control of increasingly large portions of territory and was never again as powerful.

It was during the Mughal period that the East India Company first began trading with India. Initially this was difficult for the simple reason that England had so little to offer. In 1616 Roe noted that to be taken seriously as an envoy in so opulent a place as Jahangir's court involved an enormous amount of gifts. The string of pearls and assorted other items he presented paled into insignificance beside the

'hundred thousand pounds of jewels', thirty-six elephants (two covered in beaten gold panels) and 'fifty
horses richly furnished' given by others. When Roe
presented Mercator's atlas of the world, then the most
up to date map available, it was simply returned as
useless. India was nothing more than blank space to
European minds.

As the Mughal Empire limped towards the 19th
century the East India Company assumed ever greater
power. In 1857, when Indian units of the Company's
private army mutinied, the British government took
direct control and the Raj began.

8

Chaos by Consent

Missing Afghanistan meant missing a significant portion of Coryate's route. He had gone directly east from Kerman, through what is now Helmand province to Herat, then the frontier of the Mughal Empire. From here he had headed east to Quetta before continuing to Agra. The alternative led south through the Baluchi desert to the Pakistani border, then north to Quetta.

All along the single road that led from Kerman through the Payeh mountains, across the southern end of the vast Dasht-e Lut desert to the ruins of Bam, I wondered what Afghanistan would have been like. In Bam, where every second house was still a pile of rubble, I had a clue.

From there to the border the mountainous desert of Iran's Baluchistan province engulfed the world. An unconquerable wilderness of forgotten ranges and stinging sand the size of Germany, spreading east and separating the Persian heartland from the kinder landscapes of the Punjab. The Hindu Kush to the north, and the Baluchi desert that went south almost to the sea, had been a barrier between Persian and India for millennia.

Afghanistan was a barely controlled quagmire of tribal allegiances and factional rivalry with a daily litany of death and destruction in the international press. Throw in a few kidnappings and I already knew that such a place was not for me. My already grey-haired mother was waiting at home for news and I pre-ferred that she got it from my letters rather than from a lurid headline. And I could not hope to be as lucky as Coryate, who had been on the wrong end of a headline at the beginning of his trip, only to be resurrected.

For a couple of months London resounded to the news of his death, published in a pamphlet – the 17th-century equivalent of newspapers – and written by a man with whom Coryate had previously clashed. John Taylor, the 'Water Poet' as he styled himself, lamented Coryate's fictitious drowning as a pretext to keep the previous spat alive. Taylor was a London boatman – the taxi drivers of their day – and took after Coryate as an exponent of Jacobean comedy. Taylor's work ran to a series of knock-about tales in the tradition of physical comedy, often with a fair amount of bawdy humour thrown in. All but one of his adventures were confined to British shores and several owed an obvious debt to Coryate. His *Penniless Pilgrimage* from London to York in 1618 both mocked and saluted Coryate; less derivative perhaps was Taylor's two-day voyage on the Thames, accomplished in a brown-paper boat with oars made of fish, and for company a man who couldn't swim. Needless to say the boat sank.

Odcombe's Complaint, the comical pamphlet mourning Coryate's death, was apparently a success because a few months later Taylor published another resurrecting him. The title, *The 8th Wonder of the World, or Coryate's Escape from his Supposed Drowning* showed that, even with Coryate abroad, others could make both sport and money out of him.

⤜

Taftan was the first stop on the Pakistani side of a border that was just a line in the sand. There was now no point in cycling until I met up with Coryate again at Quetta, 600 miles away, so the bus which left here each evening seemed the best option. Until I saw it, that is. The bus was a battered cylinder like an abandoned aircraft fuselage on wheels, full of cracked Perspex windows.

Feeling there was no alternative I bought a ticket to Quetta, and even left the border on this bus, although my spirits sank when we stopped after just a few hundred yards. The tatty interior was then filled with vegetables and cans of butter by men in dirty *shalwar kameez*, two of whom then had a punch-up outside. A crowd formed as they scuffled in the dust, encircling them only to watch, not to intervene, in the way of a school playground. The only other remaining passenger on the bus joined me at the window and we looked on through warped purple Perspex. He pointed to the smaller of the two men involved in the fight, who he said was the driver, now walking away with a bloody nose. He leant across and scrutinised the scene again, tapping thoughtfully at the window to indicate the driver's appointment. 'That man,' – he was dabbing his lip with a dirty shirt cuff – 'he is the co-driver.'

I abandoned the bus, retrieved the bicycle from the roof and made for the town's only hotel. In the morning the manager called a friend of his who knew someone who knew someone with a taxi, and although 600 miles by cab sounds extravagant, the price was actually very reasonable. In any case it wasn't so much a taxi as a pick-up truck with a spare seat.

The driver, Haji Muhammad Azam, an ex-civil

servant, arrived punctually at nine and we set off directly. The ride was going to take all day, he said, and lead us the entire length of southern Afghanistan, a potentially dangerous area at the best of times. Haji Muhammad was keen to get going as there were several checkpoints, both official and perhaps also unofficial, any one of which could cause delays. And that was without problems with the road itself, which was liable periodically to be swamped by the restless desert.

Haji Muhammad looked at the dwindling squalor of Taftan as we drove away, saying without a hint of irony that the town's name meant a kind of brightly coloured silk. I made a note of this, much to Haji Muhammad's amusement, and looked the word up later, much to mine. He was right too: this unpleasant little place had been the source of the English word 'taffeta', the type of silk used for the best ball gowns.

Outside Taftan we were suddenly in the desert, as if like me the road couldn't wait to be away. Two checkpoints later Haji Muhammad relaxed a little and put on the radio. We were on the way to the tune of happy Iranian music, careering along the smooth tarmac making good progress to the village of Nok Kundi, a 40° festival of flies. Here we had an early lunch as Haji Muhammad said he preferred to push on later. The café we stopped at was so squalid that I couldn't bring myself to eat anything and instead sat glumly on the floor drinking *chai*. Even this was disappointing as the cup was chipped, the pot cracked and dirty, and the increasing attention of the flies quite disgusting. And as I upended the pot for the last cup, the lid fell into my bowl with a clank.

Haji Muhammad sensed my mood and explained that we had to stop here to let the car cool down; and because 'there is nothing on the way, hmmm.' He lifted his face to look along the road, repeating in a creamy baritone, 'nothing …'

All day we pushed on through the most perfect desert scenery. Butter-coloured sand dunes slumped across the road, scrubby bushes cowered in the hot wind and in the distance the horizon was a parade of contorted crags and shattered peaks. On the road a quicksilver mirage retreated in front of us.

It was in a similarly harsh wilderness that Coryate experienced one of the wonderfully serendipitous coincidences that travel sometimes generates. Swaying towards him through the desert was another caravan, a private venture headed by none other than Robert Sherley, returning from India. Sherley had been dispatched as Persian ambassador to the Mughal court in another unsuccessful attempt to rally support against The Turk. He had found Emperor Jahangir hospitable enough, although beset with his own domestic problems, not least an unruly son and possible attack from the south.

The coincidence of the meeting became all the more enjoyable for Coryate when Sherley took out the *Crudities*, neatly bound and safely kept in his luggage. The two men obviously talked because Coryate reported later that Sherley had promised an introduction to Shah Abbas, should he pass through Persia again. As a parting gesture Sherley's wife, the Armenian, gave him 40 shillings, an amount that went some way to recouping what had been stolen in Diyarbakir.

Much later in the day Haji Muhammad stopped in the middle of nowhere to pray. While he did so beside a small whitewashed shrine no larger than a grave stone, I drank more *chai* and watched the first tendrils of sunset creep into the sky. Before me a mountain range slowly became a black void against the ruby sky.

'Six fifteen in front of the Koh-I-Ras mountains.' said Haji Muhammad appearing beside me. 'Note it,' he said with a smile.

I noted it and we sat in companionable silence with another pot of *chai*. Above us the light trickled away and the sky slowly changed to indigo. The same sky that covered all of Pakistan and Afghanistan and ran across Iran, and covered every country on Coryate's route all the way back to England. An impassive borderless unification that exposed political borders as the unnecessary, egotistical things they are. Why shouldn't a person be free to travel as far as they wanted? Why shouldn't our only limitation be how far we can walk in a day, or a month? Why shouldn't natural boundaries like rivers, mountains or deserts be the only impediments, as they were for our ancestors when they travelled beneath the *dyeu-s*, their shining deity?

The sound of Muhammad slamming the car door broke the spell.

↬

In the morning it was difficult to remember where I was until I looked out of the window. Even then the confusion didn't end quickly. Quetta is a frontier town, perhaps *the* frontier town of British India, and it was still a place that felt close to the edge. Neither did walking around town improve this sense of dislocation. The journey from Iran had been too quick and

Pakistan was too different, and on top of that I was beginning to feel ill.

The feeling of people being involved in some form of constructive activity, which had mitigated the chaos of Iranian streets, seemed absent here, replaced with life that was unintelligible. In the main these streets were peopled by the Pashtun, or Pathans, the outlandish bearded tribesmen who made up the majority in this area. The same ferocious tribesmen who had given the British Raj such a hard time during the 19th century and who were never really conquered. Stalemate was the best the Raj achieved, and British policy towards the Pashtuns became a litmus of British imperial attitudes. Benjamin Disraeli, the Conservative Prime Minister of the 1870s, favoured what became called the 'forward policy' in which the Empire extended its influence beyond the Indus into Afghan territory. Disraeli's approach was in response to the strengthening Russian position in Central Asia, then felt to be a threat to British interests. The Liberal Gladstone, who followed Disraeli as Prime Minister, favoured a less confrontational containment policy using the line of the Indus as an approximate barrier. At different times, depending on who was in power, the British army was either repulsed from this area, regained it, lost the Khyber

Pass or controlled it, fought the Afghans or made peace with them.

Finally in 1893 Mortimer Durand, Imperial India's Foreign Secretary, mapped out a border between British India and the Afghan tribes which ultimately bore his name, the Durand Line. With this agreed, modern Afghanistan came into being, although as with the British defined borders in Kashmir, and the creation of two Pakistans at independence, the Durand Line created as many problems as it solved.

Something of this precarious history was reflected on Quetta's streets, both in the variety of ethnic groups represented and in the form of nihilistic individualism that prevailed. It was palpable in the way people drove, crossed roads, moved: even mundane actions somehow held an implicit threat. Quetta was shot through with a true border town feel, a kind of stateless limbo that manifested itself in this barely suppressed lawlessness.

Six months before my visit, in March, during *Ashura* – the Shia festival to mark the death of Ali – a Sunni suicide bomber had killed forty-four people in a Shia mosque. This came after one of Pakistan's worst sectarian bloodbaths in July of the previous year when fifty people where killed, again in a nearby mosque during prayers.

But Quetta was almost impossible to police because of that ethnic smorgasbord. Beside the huge, barrel-chested Pashtuns were smaller round-faced Turkmen nomads, fresh from northern Afghanistan as refugees; and beside them smooth-skinned Sunni Punjabis from further east as well as Hazaras, Baluchis, Mohajirs and Sindhis. The only underrepresented group on the streets was women.

⌒

Osman was a bicycle courier who wheezed as he spoke. He had pointed out some of the differing ethnic groups as we chatted, starting with himself, a Punjabi, although he was preoccupied with other more personal matters.

'Things are so bad here,' he said when I asked about cycling in such a town. 'But you can get used to it.' Life was much better in the Punjab but he had come here to work and study and made do as best he could. He delivered medicines to the various surgeries in and around Jinnah Road, the main thoroughfare, and spent six days a week cycling. He was on his rounds now and couldn't stop, so he suggested meeting later.

'We will have dinner together,' he said with a hopeful confidence; but when we met he was morose.

'I will come with you but I can eat nothing.' He rolled his eyes. 'I am not feeling so well lately.' The wind, which had blown constantly that day, had died down by this time releasing the quite incredible smell of the city's drains. I wasn't feeling so well myself in the face of this stench and as a precaution we went to one of the better restaurants.

I ordered the blandest thing possible, boiled rice and vegetables, and bottled water. Osman looked at the menu and blanched. He rubbed his eyes complaining of a headache and repeated his refusal to eat. He would just have cola, he said, and spoke to the waiter at length. It was not American cola, he stressed turning back to me, it was made in Pakistan. He didn't hold with the capitalism of the West and saw non-Asian companies as exploitative. The Islamic world was showing the way in this respect and he was pleased that Pakistan was playing a part. I began to ask how such companies were structured if not in the same way as western companies, but Osman wasn't listening. It was better not to dilute the teachings of the Koran, he said with blank sincerity. As an Islamic republic Pakistan had much to contribute in this way.

'In fact', he said, perking up a little, 'science has now shown how Islam was right all the way.'

Using the fingers to eat with, he said glossing

over the universality of this, was preferable because oils from the fingers improved digestion. And the ablutions performed before prayers encouraged good hygiene, while the actions of the prayers themselves promoted a basic level of fitness within the community.

'And looking at opposite sex naked is also bad – science has now proved this. It damages eyesight.'

I put my drink down.

'Sorry, science has proved ... ? '

'... that looking at naked women is bad for eyesight. Study in Switzerland has shown it. It is on internet.'

I pondered this as Osman reached out a hand towards the menu.

He went on with the religious theme. 'You know, body is hardware, soul is software.' Then triumphantly: 'And religion is manual.'

He seemed a little happier after this and continued in the same vein while scrutinising the menu.

Life was an exam; those who passed went to Paradise, those who failed went to 'the hill'. And within Paradise there were levels, just like the grades of an exam. In Paradise everything was perfect. There were rivers of honey and, 'you just need to think of the most delicious food and it is in your mouth. There is no bowel in paradise, and no urine. Everything is perfect. And there are many women.' He couldn't restrain a smirk.

'You mean for pleasure?'

'Yes, yes,' he nodded, 'but this is not sin, it is reward. And you can eat pork without damage to the brain.' Science had apparently also proved that eating pork led to brain damage.

Osman called the waiter over and they spoke at length once more.

'What if you're married?' I asked. 'Won't your wife be angry if you carry on with these women?'

'No, of course not. I told you, everything is perfect.'

'Where do the women come from? Were they good women during their lives? What if your wife qualifies for a higher level of paradise than you, will there be men for her?'

Osman ignored this and went back to the computer metaphor. Software manuals were always being revised, he said, the latest version being the best. Like any manual the Koran included information on the old versions, Christianity and Judaism.

'Koran has reference to previous prophets Ibrahim and Issa [Jesus] – so it is proved: Islam is the latest version.' He looked at me sympathetically.

I said, 'What about the Sikh holy book, didn't that come after the Koran?'

But Osman had drifted off again. He was gazing lovingly at an old man who was praying on a mat near our table. I had also had my eye on the man because he was blocking access to the toilet, which I now needed quite badly.

'Oh, he is a very good man,' cooed Osman, 'very good man.'

My food arrived, followed by the dishes Osman had finally found the strength to order. It was good to eat healthily, he said picking up a fork and looking disparagingly at my rice.

During the meal his conversation returned to the concept of paradise, and specifically to the women in Paradise, generally at first but then in an increasingly prurient fashion. In the end I had to change the subject, although this didn't bother Osman at all. He switched seamlessly to how rich the West was and rambled about how he would work there one day. He was studying for an MSc in Pharmacology, a good profession and one he could use if he ever did leave Pakistan.

When the bill came Osman gave a final flourish about rich westerners and allowed me to pay.

'You are a good man,' he said, and rolled his bovine eyes.

We said goodbye on the pavement outside and I walked unsteadily back to the hotel, where I was copiously sick in the bathroom.

↝

Feeling a little fragile the next day, I walked the short distance to the railway station, looking for a list of Brits who died in the 1935 earthquake. Almost the whole city had been flattened at the time and the list I found was of railway employees, around 150 of whom died that day.

While I was walking around the rest of the station, taking in some of the left over trappings of colonialism, I couldn't resist poking my head into the First Class Air Con (Gents) waiting room, where there was an ancient copy of *The Times* on the table. I had just started reading this when a man bustled in and demanded to know where I was going. I was ready to leave, thinking that he must be an inspector of some sort, when it transpired that he was a passenger. After his blustering show of familiarity with foreigners he took one of the room's two day-beds and fell asleep almost at once, in a way I was to become familiar with on the subcontinent. I had just spread the paper on the small table when the man began snoring loudly, then farting and finally fondling his goolies, all without waking. I repositioned myself to avoid seeing this and continued with the paper until an older man with a hennaed beard and lace skull-cap came into the room. He sank into the other day-bed and within minutes he too was asleep and handling his genitals.

I quit the room and went along the platform for *chai* and biscuits. Just before I reached the stall there was a commotion from a side gate and I was barged aside by a harassed-looking policeman.

'Make way, make way,' he puffed, 'Minister is coming, Minister of Stations.'

He bustled to the waiting room and spun like a ballerina, snapping to attention beside the door. Through the gate came a small portly man in black, with dyed black hair and a black hat resembling a fez. He was preceded by a gabbling entourage of administrators rather like sheep being herded by an overweight collie. Army radios crackled, people ran randomly about and all normal business on the plat-form ceased. The minister swung into the waiting room, which was then sealed off, separating me from my bag and the newspaper. Luckily the Minister merely inspected the small, bare, room and swept out again, this time with the entourage behind him like a crowd scene in a low-budget movie.

A little bemused I went back to the waiting room and put my head through the door, hoping to see what had been of such great ministerial interest. Apart from the table, a brown box on the wall containing the Koran, and the two day-beds, there was nothing. And on the beds lay the same two men, still asleep and still groping themselves.

～

A few days later in Multan, in the Punjab, at St Mary's church in the cantonment district I met doctors Samuel Khokhar and Ahsen Mian, Christian and Muslim respectively, sitting under a tree on the *chowkidar*'s (caretaker's) lawn. The two doctors collaborated in an NGO and were currently developing a project to save the Indus dolphin, the most endangered cetacean species in the world according to Dr Khokhar. The population had been as low as a hundred during the Seventies when industrial pollution controls were minimal and agricultural pesticide washed off every field. Since then the numbers had come back up to around 500, although this was by no means healthy. The dolphin only lived in the last 120 miles of the river, not in the upper reaches, and the species was almost blind. They hunted by sound and touch in the thick sediments of the river and were sensitive to any changes in the river's ecosystem.

'These dolphins are an important part of nature here, but they also represent our commitment to looking after our environment and controlling our own affairs. There is still some left over resentment about that. Many people say that the best period here was the British time, now we have to show that we are equal on the international stage. Our NGO helps do that. You know international volunteers come here to help us count the dolphins.'

Multan had been a centre for industry for many hundreds of years. It was on the main caravan route from Persia since the 15th century, although the city is much older. In the 1660s when the French traveller François Bernier came through the Mughal Empire he recorded that after Agra, Lahore, Ajmer and Delhi, Multan was the wealthiest Mughal city. One of the Mughal mints was located here during the 16th and 17th centuries and the habit of trade had stuck. Business had been put first in Multan since the 16th century, Dr Mian said, when agriculture along the banks of the Indus had intensified to feed the ever growing population.

'But always that comes at the expense of the environment; now we want to change the balance a little with our organisation.'

One of the NGO's other projects was to bring cleaner drinking water to Multan. 'There is so much pollution it even effects what we eat and drink,' Dr Khokhar said.

Industrial and agricultural pollution was so prevalent that it couldn't be kept out of the water table and had contaminated drinking water supplies.

The *chowkidar*'s son bought tea out to us on a tray and laid it on the small garden table. He was studying agriculture in Multan and hoped to become an advisor to the government once he had qualified. He too shared the doctors' view that it was time to do something about Pakistani environmental issues: it was time to join the world community in this way. Of course the Pakistani economy wasn't as good as it could be, and in some respects the country was in a kind of 'industrial dark age', as he put it, but this shouldn't stop someone at least trying to do something.

We sipped our tea for a while and watched a bird the size of a large dove, with zebra stripes, orange shoulders and the most extraordinary quiff, butt its head into the turf.

'But this country is not safe for you I think.' Dr Khokhar said, musing on the bird. 'We have many problems with religion here. Even this morning I heard an explosion. I don't know what, but it sounded like a bomb.'

This was not an exaggeration. At around seven o'clock that morning a car bomb had killed forty Sunnis as they left an all-night prayer gathering in the suburbs. Two minutes later in the ensuing mêlée, a second bomb strapped to a parked motorcycle went off.

We all went back to looking at the bird. Its beak and the ruff at the back of its head were so evenly proportioned that it looked like a kind of feathered hammer. The *chowkidar*'s son threw some bread and the bird hopped to within a few feet of us.

I said, 'I suppose you feed it all the time?'

'No indeed not,' the doctors said in unison. 'We don't usually feed the birds,' Dr Mian went on, 'there is enough natural food for them. He is very trusting.'

✑

In Multan I had at last caught up with Coryate. His letters had been silent about Quetta and it had been a long time since there had been anything more than a few words from him. In Multan, however, Coryate was back with a vengeance. All the way from Turkey he had more or less kept his own counsel, making his way and writing his notes, but producing nothing in that time in the way of letters. I knew that it had taken him four months between Esfahan and Lahore, with no detail recorded other than the meeting with Robert Sherley.

Again it is inconceivable that Coryate was not recording every detail. The letters, full and forth-right as they are in some respects, seem to be holding something back. They are not as anecdotal as they could be, and certainly much less detailed than the material Purchas had from him on Constantinople. Coryate gives his route, makes a couple of biblical references, quotes Plato and, touchingly, tells his mother, 'I would have you know that I always go safely', although he then goes on to tell her he will not be home for at least another four years. To his friends he can't resist name-dropping the Mughal Emperor Jahangir, and finally, in the second letter to his mother dated October 1616 – a year before his death – he relates a somewhat manic outburst in Multan, a tirade, 'against Muhammad and his accursed religion'.

He proudly recalls meeting an Italian Muslim in the city, and that the man had the temerity to call Coryate an unbeliever. He responded in Italian with an abusive monologue that owed something both to

210

the harangues of his court days and to an obvious frustration with his long months in Muslim lands. He held forth in no small way on how Muhammad was no more than a merchant who married well; how he conned people, 'partly by a tame pigeon that did fly to his eare for meat [food]'; and how Coryate was 'perswaded thou wouldst spit in the face of thy Alcaron [Koran] ... and bury it under a jaxe [toilet]'.

He goes on in the same vein, heaping scorn on Muhammad, ridiculing the Muslim notion of Paradise ('full of stinking dung hills') and declaring that Muhammad 'himselfe was a man of very superficiall and mean learning'. Coryate had already written two books better than the Koran, he informs his hapless victim, 'and will hereafter this (by Gods gracious permission) write another better and truer'.

Coryate doesn't relate what happened next, leaving us to assume the wretch slunk off with his tail between his legs. Although he does at least have the decency to admit that it was only the tolerance of Mughal society that allowed him to escape this outburst with his life.

'If I had spoken thus much in Turkey or Persia against Mohomet, they would have roasted me upon a spit.'

Coryate finishes the letter by telling his mother

that he has, 'resolved to write no more while I am in these mahometans countries'. He would rather wait until he was nearer home before announcing himself, no doubt the better to burst on an unsuspecting public.

9

The Long Walk

At Lahore Coryate entered the last phase of his journey. The Mughal Empire was one of the safer places he had visited, so he parted company with the caravan and travelled alone to Agra, the Mughal capital. The journey was made easier by the Mughal creation of what British merchants called the 'Long Walk', one of the most striking roads anywhere in the world at the time. Coryate records that for 20 days he walked, 'through such a delicate and even tract of ground as I never saw before'. And through that ground, now the Punjab province, ran a tree-lined avenue that stretched for 200 miles. 'A row of trees on each side of this way where people do travel, extending itself from the town's end of Lahore to the town's end of Agra.'

This Long Walk was part of the trade route spanning northern India, linking Calcutta in the east with Kabul 1,500 miles away in the west. The route had been in existence for centuries when, 300 years after Coryate, Kipling wrote of what was then called the Grand Trunk road, '... such a river of life as nowhere else exists in the world.'

It was still that and more when I cycled along it another hundred years later. It was the most crowded, noisy, polluted, chaotic, exultant, vital stretch of road I'd ever seen. All India seemed to be here pounding along the tarmac, and all India's history represented beside it in the villages, the shrines, the ancient battlefields and the modern cities that pressed together in the flat green farmland. At times it was the easiest cycling possible. The temperature had dropped to a comfortable level, there were roadside *chai* stalls every few kilometres and the road was flat and smooth. On the other hand there was every type of animal to contend with, from a flock of geese to goats, cows, donkeys, dogs; even a camel that had broken its tether and was running between the lanes of traffic with graceful slow-motion strides.

And then there was the traffic itself. Being a cyclist in India was like being subject to a form of torture by noise. The 'GT' road, as this acronym-obsessed nation knows it, was a constant barrage of blaring horns assaulting the air from morning to night. A sort of caste system applied to roads, with trucks at the top and the lowly cyclist at the bottom; and I was told by an ancient man in a roadside *chai* shop that it was compulsory to use the horn when overtaking, so as everyone overtakes the cyclist it becomes his lot to suffer in this way.

This same road, as the Long Walk, became a prominent feature when Sir Thomas Roe produced the first English map of India in 1619. Some of the information in the map, as well as the inclusion of the Long Walk, was undoubtedly down to Coryate. Of the few Englishmen who had passed along it he was the only one then in India and he was certainly the only one to have gone north into the Himalayan foothills, which he did on a walking tour in 1617. Although, true to form, Coryate's contribution went uncredited. Perhaps his input explains why Roe's map shows north India greatly exaggerated, Coryate's loquacious enthusiasm enough even to influence the proportions of a country.

⤻

The large and slightly dilapidated old villa housing the Indian Council of Historical Research was at the heart of Lutyens' New Delhi, equidistant between Connaught Circus and India Gate. I was directed to the first floor office of the deputy director, Mr Sudhir

Anand, by an ancient man in a blue checked *dhoti* and a grimy white singlet.

The office was a cosy place full of paper and files and Mr Anand a busy but helpful man.

'We have the type of book you are looking for,' he said matter-of-factly as he swept a pair of heavy glasses from his nose.

'But you must understand that the process of history is somewhat political in India.' The glasses went into his top pocket in a single movement. 'Many of these books are old and need conserving and so you will have to be careful. They date from before independence and are by European authors. They are considered colonial and therefore less of a priority for conservation. Although the information they contain is often perfectly valid.'

It was a problem with wider implications, Mr Anand told me. The Indian Council of Historical Research had been set up at the behest of Indira Gandhi in the Seventies and had been given the job of writing a new history of India. There had previously been a famous history of India written by two Englishmen, a biased and pessimistic account implying that Indian self-government would never work. Mrs Gandhi wanted to set the record straight and wanted this new history to be the first written by Indians.

'The book is to be called *Towards Freedom*. It was supposed to be in 17 volumes,' Mr Anand said dolefully hitching at his shirt under his jacket.

'In 2001 – it took that long – the first two volumes were at the printers when they were pulled. Someone in government had read them and decided they did not favour the Hindus enough. This person also did not like the Communist Party getting such a positive write-up and said the council had been infiltrated by Marxists. Remember this was 2001, the height of the BJP Hindu revival. The government wanted to have a more "saffronised" version of Indian history, so they ordered the whole series to be reviewed.

'Nothing has come of that project so far. All the research and all the effort will have been wasted if nothing is done. And there are counter-rumours that the government is also infiltrated by Marxists.' He laughed in private amusement.

'But you know we have a generally good experience of communism here, unlike Europe. To us communism is an experiment that is not over. Everywhere you find communists in public life. Not campaigning or political communists, just people who favour that approach. The same way you find Christians in Britain.'

Mr Anand took me along a couple of institutionally

drab corridors past filing cabinets and boxes of paper, down some stairs to the 'library-cum-documentation centre'.

'I must leave you here I fear,' he said, his mobile phone ringing inside his jacket. He nodded at the librarian to indicate I should be signed in. We said goodbye and I watched him walk along the corridor. From the back he looked like a chair with a jacket hung over it.

The library was a bibliophile's dream. There wasn't a computer in sight, only row upon dingy row of musty books in grey cabinets. And there was even a separate sub-section titled 'Travel – 17th century – European'. I had found the motherlode. Dozens of books dealing with exactly the subject area I had become obsessed with. Two shelves of titles like *Early English Adventurers in the East*, and *Early Travels in India*, or *Bombay and Western India, a Series of Stray Papers*. But my excitement quickly ebbed away as I examined them. One by one it became obvious, with the slow inevitability of a rising tide, that not a single book contained anything new. Each one reworked the same information about Coryate from a slightly different perspective. And neither was there one reference to the missing notes, nor any hint of what they contained or what might have happened to them.

The books were compilations and edited collections concentrating almost exclusively on merchants. The only exceptions were religious men like Edward Terry, who had been the English ambassador Sir Thomas Roe's chaplain in India, and who in any case had travelled in support of merchants. Only in one or two places did Coryate appear, and when he did there was much chewing over old news.

The most interesting text I found was an anacdote showing the struggle Coryate faced was not only physical but also social. A merchant called Richard Steel had arrived in Mandu, where Coryate spent some time and where I would be heading next. The two men were apparently pleased to see eachother, both because their caravans had crossed paths when Coryate arrived in India and also because Steel had been home in the meantime and had news from court. But if Coryate expected reports of an adoring public clamouring for his next book he was disappointed. Steel said only that when he told King James of his meeting with Coryate, the King had replied: 'Is the fool still living?' A throwaway comment from a monarch but one at which Coryate took umbrage. He had come so far and achieved so much that to be dismissed in this way was too much. The Great Walk and the last five years of his life had accomplished

nothing: he was still the fool, part of the entertain-
ment and no more than a servant.

I left the library rather dejectedly and went back to
my hotel. There was nothing new to find on Coryate.
My best hope had been Delhi, the administrative heart
of this paper-loving bureaucracy. There was to be no
golden pot. But at least the afternoon had given me
the chance to get a behind the scenes look at Indian
bureaucracy, which in itself was an interesting experience and one that had rather changed my view of it.

On the surface, which was the part most visitors
saw, government departments could be chaotic. They
could be officious and yet at the same time operate
in almost geological slow-motion. In fact merely
chaotic was the best of it – a little disorganisation
at a ticket window in a country of a billion seemed
forgivable. At worst the Indian bureaucratic machine
could appear apathetic and at times even vengeful and
so one of the most edifying aspects of my search for
Coryate was that it took me behind the scenes. I was
able to get away from the harassed bank clerks and
hotel staff and talk to people who didn't usually meet
foreigners. Expert librarians, seasoned archaeologists, historians. People who toiled at the heart of the
colossal Indian machine, recording, classifying and
cataloguing; knocking the enormity of Indian history

into shape. People who invited me into their offices and called me Mr Daniel *Ji* – Daniel Sir. Meetings that were wonderfully soothing interruptions to the bedlam of India.

Trailing Coryate gave the excuse to call on these people and quiz them about what they knew. And without exception they were helpful, although I never once made an appointment and often didn't know who to speak to when I arrived. People came out of meetings to help, gave up their lunch breaks and were unfailingly polite in doing so.

～

The Indias that Coryate and I came to were Indias of different worlds and the journeys we made separated by the gulf of colonialism. It was almost impossible now to see India in the way Coryate had seen it. British India – quintessential colonialism – divided us in a way that was difficult to overcome. In the post-colonial world of re-examination and redress it was difficult to be in India and not feel a little guilt. So much of India's modern consciousness was connected either with the Raj, or the wish to be rid of it, that it was difficult to imagine a time when India did not exist in relation to Britain.

'The East is a career,' was the kind of phrase that

was often heard at the height of the British colonial period, and to many merchants it was to become just that. The Victorian love of nostalgic history made their Orientalism particularly strong, and although their interest in the east was partly cultural, it was also a function of their wish to control it (it was Disraeli after all who made Queen Victoria 'Empress of India').

The point to be made here is that Coryate came before today's post-colonial culture and all it contains. He pre-dated, for example, that now ubiquitous comment on colonialism, Conrad's *Heart of Darkness*. Coryate's own voyage to the heart of a continent, and the heart of an empire, did not lead him to a heart of darkness. Instead he found the chaotic, sun-jangled hugger-mugger of a vivid subcontinent. Neither did the first colonialists after Coryate find their Kurtz in India's dusty interior. Rather they found happy wives, history to rival the Mediterranean, mellifluous languages, complex and virtually unknown religions and the art that went with them.

Coryate's own 'voyage upstream' into India subverts what had not yet come, but what has since become our viewpoint. There was no terrible savagery at the core, revealed by the paring blade of travel; no native to return to and no animal to become. That was all later. Coryate's was a trip of innocence in this respect. In his day the Afghan wars that made the Khyber Pass a household name, and the Raj civil servants who bought home the words 'bungalow', 'pyjama' and 'shampoo' were all in the future. The glory and the discomfiture of empire was still to come.

As the Orient began gently to dissolve into the English consciousness, so society began to reflect this new world. Coryate was exposed to the first years of this new phenomenon at court in London where he would have seen the general interest that was the first stirrings of colonialism in England. But Coryate's methodical, empirical voice was soon swept away. Commerce made men loquacious. Business success bought ever more florid eulogies, and with each new success, commercialising the relationship between East and West, the balance of power began to change. Europe began again to have the upper hand. Trade, and the pursuit of it, was more than just a career; it was the making of Great Britain.

Being British seemed to give me a head start in India, where so many people spoke English, the infrastructure was recognisable and where personal behaviour could be dictated by caste identity. And the landscape too was familiar in its agricultural patterns, its rhythms, its network of villages, its ancient social order.

Roe's map illustrated Coryate's indirect role in the vanguard of colonialism. At a time when the English public was just becoming interested in the Orient as a phenomenon, Coryate was in the East as the only independent traveller. So important was it at the time to have first-hand information that Lord Carew, a senior member of the government, entreated Roe, 'to be careful to make the map of the Mughal's territory', and encouraged him with the opinion that once complete the map would, 'leave to the world a lasting memory when you are dust.'

It is unfair to say that Coryate too played a part in the colonial process. Unfair because he chose specifically to avoid the colonial mission. He was not a merchant; he was free of this influence and the pressures that came with it. He was representing no one but himself and was under no obligation to trade, to expand English influence or territory, or to proselytise. He was in fact extremely un-colonial in comparison to every other foreigner then abroad in the world. His journey to the East was made in an Age-of-Reason spirit of investigation; the same spirit and approach that persisted into the Enlightenment.

Was it too much to see a little of that pioneering courage and energy in, for example, Darwin's voyages? He like Coryate was a product of his age, using the intellectual tools of his day drawn from a particular field of study, in his case zoology. The practical approach which led Coryate to travel, led Darwin to his own voyages and his own conclusions. They were both men who built on the renaissance mission of experience and went to see for themselves, using the human instinct for travel to fuel their investigations.

∽

Ajmer Fort was a tall quadrangle of square stone topped with a roof terrace that had an ornate cupola at each corner. In the courtyard inside, a square stone building served as a museum, although this was closed. In fact the fort itself had been closed the previous day and the opening hours were unclear, seemingly masked in a bureaucratic fog. Where rules and regulations were concerned India could sometimes overcomplicate things to the point where official regulations seemed more like deliberate disinformation.

In frustration at this, and the lack of anyone to talk to about the fort's history, I went 'Bumbling'. It was a trick I'd used before. Like the 'Bunberrying' of *The Importance of Being Ernest*, Bumbling gives you scope. You start in the public areas of whichever place you're in – the station concourse, the museum café, whatever the location has to offer – then you nip through a likely-looking door into the privacy beyond. If you bump into someone you play the tourist and say, 'I'm sorry, I seem to be lost', and make a hasty exit, all the while protected by the conventions of politeness and hospitality.

Opening a door at the fort led into a cool limestone corridor punctuated by heavy wooden doors. All of these were locked and so I went to the end of the corridor where it widened out into a larger room with a groin vaulted ceiling. This was where I met Monmohan, the fort's caretaker, a delightful man in his early thirties who was not the slightest bit surprised to see me. He continued pottering about his morning's chores, tending to the fire and cooking lunch for himself and his beautiful albino daughter Ajanta. Had I come far to see the fort, he asked as some people had previously come from England because of its importance in colonial history.

Monmohan had been educated in Delhi and come to work here four years ago. He wanted a change in life and somewhere stable for his daughter to grow up. They had come to enjoy living at the fort although Ajmer was a busy city. He found it peaceful to have so much solid stone between him and the traffic outside.

We walked out into the courtyard again, into the sunlight where Ajanta danced in and out of the doorway. We chatted for a few minutes until finally Ajanta pulled at her father's sleeve. Could we go back inside, she asked, the light was uncomfortable. We continued our conversation back in the shade where the earthy tang of the stonework filled the room.

The fortress had been built in 1570 by Akbar as the royal residence in Ajmer, then an important regional city because of its proximity to troublesome Rajasthan. Since then it had been used for peaceful purposes rather than as an active fort. It was in the heart of the old city, surrounded by colour and chaos that can't have looked very different 400 years ago.

Coryate had come here directly from Agra, in July 1615 when he learnt that Jahangir was here. In May of that year an outbreak of plague had gripped the Punjab and both Delhi and Agra were affected. In the circumstances they were not places to linger and so Coryate made the ten-day walk south onto the ramparts of the Western Highlands.

Once he reached Ajmer, the Great Walk from the Holy Land to India was at last over, in as much as any journey could be over for a permanent traveller. A journey that Coryate measured at 2,700 'English' miles although in fact the distance was more like 3,500 miles. The error comes because the mile had not been standardised at that time, and in any case all three Islamic empires used their own units of measurement; the Mughal *kos* being something like two English miles. Whatever the exact distance, walking had taken the – to my mind – remarkably short time of nine months, taking into account the four months in Aleppo and two in Esfahan.

In Ajmer Coryate joined the small number of English merchants then present in the town, and settled down for a long and well earned rest. He spent the next 14 months as guest of the indulgent merchants, 'not spending one little piece of money', to his great delight. How he spent his days here is unknown but a fair bet is that he wrote up the third set of notes, made since Esfahan.

Coryate does record that he made good progress learning Persian and that he had also picked up some Hindi. Perhaps somehow conscious of his role as the 'first backpacker', and in the spirit of mass tourism that was to follow, he also took a ride on an elephant. He was impressed enough that he determined 'one day (by God's leave) to have my picture expressed in my next book sitting upon an elephant'. In respect of this wish the four letters published in 1616 under the title *Traveller for the English Wits*, had Coryate resplendent in full Jacobean dress and spurs riding a rather peevish elephant.

Coryate also took the time to record one or two local customs in the letters, emphasising what a mine of information the lost book would have been. Again what he records is detailed and accurate, and in its way typical of the oddball Coryate. The man whose European trip gave Britain the distinction of knowing exactly when it started using the fork, provides us with another bizarrely interesting piece of information: the exact weight of a 17th-century emperor.

Jahangir, Coryate tells us, was in the habit of dispensing alms to the poor on his birthday and had adopted a novel, and actually quite ancient, way of doing this. Amid much ceremony and public attention Jahangir sat 'in a pair of golden scales' to be weighed. An equal weight in gold was then dispensed among the poor which, in 1616, amounted to 12st, 5 lbs.

It was from Ajmer that three of Coryate's five extant letters were sent, addressing his friends in London with news from India as well as relating stories of his journey there. Letters that were the equivalent of the Purchas information for the Holy Land and Turkey, but which were in truth not as good. They compressed the journey into an itinerary and although there is some detail it merely serves to tantalise the reader.

I wondered if there was any chance of seeing where they had been written and asked Monmohan where the English residence had been.

'Some historians would like to know this also,' he said, 'but so far it has not been discovered. Thomas Roe came to the fort to meet Jahangir in January 1616, as you will see,' he pointed to the fort's impressive entrance where a plaque commemorated the visit. 'But no one knows where he stayed. It would have been a wooden house so perhaps nothing remains of it now.'

Roe had arrived in Ajmer in December 1615 having left England in March and sailed around the Cape of Good Hope. He had become ill on the voyage and was, in his own words, 'scarce a crow's dinner' by the time he arrived. Roe's incapacity – he had to be carried – didn't stop Coryate from welcoming him with a fine and no doubt lengthy oration.

The house Roe ended up in was in a compound allocated to the English merchants in which the accommodation, Roe recorded in his diary, was made of straw. He doesn't give a location but confided that he lived in constant fear of fire, which he says was a daily occurrence in the city. He would probably therefore have been in what is now the old quarter close to the fort.

As Roe had various presents to ease dealings with Jahangir, and the merchants had all their trade goods in their accommodation, a serious fire could easily have ended the British presence in India. Eventually Roe could stand it no longer and demolished the house himself in a day, which gives a clue to its condition. The industrious ambassador then set about building himself a new house of brick and plaster and had finished seven rooms within ten days.

Monmohan and I went through the three rooms that he and his daughter occupied, with high ceilings and whitewashed walls. Ajanta went into her bedroom and returned to show me a colouring book. She was doing well, Monmohan said, and would join a local school soon. Until then he would educate her.

I had wanted to get into one of the fort's third-floor rooms but Monmohan said this was impossible as they were being renovated and were unsafe. These were the private rooms where Jahangir held court and which were shielded from the world by an intricate pierced screen of stone. It was his custom to appear behind this screen, or on the ornate balcony beside it, twice a day. Here he would listen to petitions and dispense what justice or recompense he saw fit.

It was here that Coryate joined the crowd one day and presented himself to Jahangir from the street below, as was the custom. He delivered a short speech in Persian, the purpose of which, among a great many compliments, was basically to get some money from Jahangir.

Coryate had come to the end of his time in Ajmer and was preparing to leave on the next stage of his travels. He asked Jahangir if he would give a letter of safe conduct to go north to Samarkand, to which the Emperor replied that he held no sway there and so would not. The Tartars hated Christians so much, the Emperor said, that Coryate would surely be murdered if he went there. It seemed that on this advice he revised the plan and decided instead to go back home through Persia.

Coryate deliberately kept his visit to Jahangir from Roe, feeling that he would not approve and would try to interfere. Roe was trying to maintain as much dignity as possible in difficult circumstances; the last thing he wanted was Coryate loose and talking to the Emperor in Persian. Who knows what damage he might have done to English prestige? Roe made this point to Coryate, who was having none of it. He answered Roe robustly, and the ambassador 'was contented to cease nibbling at me'. Coryate was not a merchant to be ordered about, he was in India of his own choosing. He came and went as he pleased and it was not for Roe to tell him who he may or may not talk to. In any case, as Coryate writes, 'never had I more need of money in all my life.' The money that Jahangir did give, equivalent to about £10, was a relatively large amount for the penniless *fakir* (religious wanderer). In fact he was down to his last pound prior to that, which, even for Coryate, was not enough to get home.

Walking away from the fort through the crush of the bazaar I saw a solitary man in the street being passed by a long queue of traffic. He was moving slowly, rhythmically, rolling, carefully moving an alms bowl as he went. He was absolutely fearless of the grinding traffic and oblivious of the people packing the streets. Ajmer was home to the shrine of a medieval Sufi saint, a point of pilgrimage for Muslims from all over India, and the man must have been on his way there. At first I thought his rolling was purely as an act of devotion, but as he made his way past me it was obvious that he had lost both legs and that his was an act both of piety and of courage. I put some money into his bowl and he passed on wordlessly. Wherever he had come from, and however far he had travelled, he had just a few hundred yards left now.

⌒

After his extended stay in Ajmer Coryate was eager to do some more travelling and to see some of the holy sights of northern India. Jahangir had decided to move his court south and as ambassador Roe was obliged to follow, although the independent Coryate was not and so took the opportunity to walk with two of the mission's English merchants to Agra. Here he again stayed with the East India Company, this time for around three months, before setting off to visit the Himalayan foothills, the source of the Ganges at Haridwar, and the temple of Jawalamukhi Devi in Kangra district. He briefly mentions this side trip in his letters, although again the descriptions he gives amount to little more than a taste of the missing book.

From the Himalaya he returned to the factory at Agra, where in July 1617 the merchants received a letter from Roe, then in Mandu south of Ajmer. Roe's letter was of interest to Coryate too because he asks: 'will he go back to England or stay; or if I take any new course whither he will go with me'.

The new course was Persia, where Roe expected to be sent and where Coryate was in any case probably heading. Arriving there as part of an ambassador's retinue would suit Coryate, especially as he hoped that another ambassador, Robert Sherley, had already paved the way with Shah Abbas. So in late July 1617 he turned his face for Mandu a good twenty days to the south in the arid farmland of the northern Deccan.

The city had been abandoned for about 50 years when Coryate arrived, although it was substantial enough that Jahangir's vast court could still make use of the buildings.

Today Mandu is the perfect ghost city of forgotten fortresses and dusty palaces, ruined outbuildings, scrappy vegetation and emptiness, strung out along a ridge overlooking the Narmada River. The skyline is full of silhouetted pavilions, battlements, crags and the dark shapes of birds forever circling. Everywhere dilapidated buildings were being swamped by the jungle giving the stone an organic look and creating the impression of a lost kingdom.

Jahangir moved off again on 29 October followed again by Roe and Coryate. Both men must have been a little disappointed because it seems they may have been ill. Roe certainly was, and to add to his woes he had just received instructions to stay in India. English negotiations with the Mughal Empire for trading concessions were not going well, mainly because England had nothing Jahangir wanted, and Roe was now ordered to make further efforts. This meant Coryate's lift to Persia by boat was off, and, as the court broke up to move away, he may have hoped it was heading to Agra, from where he could have gone on to Lahore and joined a caravan.

Unfortunately this hope too was dashed when it was decided that the court would head instead for Ahmedabad in the west. At this point Coryate decided to cut his losses and make for Surat 200 miles away on the coast. Given his previous intention of starting his homeward journey it would seem that he had decided to find a ship at Surat, bound either for Persia, or even for England.

After five years and the best part of 4,000 miles Thomas Coryate had begun the long walk home.

10

The Truth Beneath the Tomb

The sky above Suvali is bleached to a pale blue by the sea. The high tropical sun tucks a neat black shadow beneath each tree. The air is scented with juniper and a smell that has become familiar, the smell of heat.

It took over an hour to cover the ten miles from Surat, struggling all the way into the warm, damp wind. The same wind buffeted the abandoned fields beside the road, combed through the parched grass and smeared the high cloud to chalk dust. Suvali succumbed to this wind long ago, the wind that blew across the Indian Ocean from Arabia, circling the warm sea.

Against the powder-blue of the sky the monument was a simple strong form. Inside there was a low stone bench, and carved into the plaster an indistinguishable name above the date 'June 1883'. In the apex of the dome a flash of red paint – a vaguely floral circle

– accents what must have been a lantern hook. Below, the floor is flat and smooth and the corners filled with crescents of sand. Sections of missing plaster show flat red bricks and coarse mortar beneath.

No one I'd spoken to in Surat, a city of four million, had ever heard of the monument. Even in Suvali no one knew. I spent so long on tiny sandy lanes, cycling from hamlet to hamlet, that by the time I found it I had not the slightest idea where I was. Other than I was finally exactly where I wanted to be.

England was easy to forget here in the afternoon sun of the Subcontinent. And it was easy to under-stand how Coryate could have consigned its preoc-cupations to a different world. Being in such a place, so far from home in every respect, it was almost impossible not to loose track of one's roots. Travel can be a great leveller in this respect. In the outback of Gujarat it wasn't difficult to imagine that Coryate's social status no longer mattered.

In the scrub near the monument a group of palm trees stood like a firework burst against the sky. Nearby the buffalo swung their jaws and chewed and a slim man picked his way through the undergrowth. He didn't look up and didn't notice the monument. To him the scene was never-changing, a fixture in his life like his own furniture.

He wouldn't have known the monument as Tom Coryate's Tomb either. That came from British maritime charts and had fallen out of use since independence. Navigating the Tapti River into Surat – the city that was the East India Company, and England's, first toehold in India – had always been a problem and so the tomb had been plotted onto 19th century Admiralty charts. Coryate, the pioneer, symbolically showing the way.

A coastline like this can change a great deal in a short time and Rajgiri was shown differently on almost every map. It was on a strip of the littoral marked variously as a peninsula dribbling down the coast, an island, or a bar protecting the lagoon behind. In truth the land here could be any of these depending on the season and maps that seem to contradict each other over the centuries can all be made to agree.

At the tomb there was no name and, crucially no date, other than the graffito, and that was no guide to when it had been built. There was no dedicatory cartouche or explanatory inscription to help the weary traveller. I looked everywhere but unless it was worn smooth or hidden beneath the moss I doubt it had ever existed. Without the tethering humanity of a name and a date the monument belonged more to the landscape than to any individual, and with that link to Coryate absent I felt that I was a stranger there.

I went back to Surat and thankfully the journey was easier, both because of the wind and because everyone knew where Surat was. A couple of miles from Rajgiri the vast skeleton of a gas refinery cluttered the southern skyline. In the next village, which was just a break of shops, two good hotels and an international telephone kiosk showed how a natural gas strike meant largesse at a local level as well as benefit at the national.

I rode back into Surat at increasing speed, swept along by the mania for overtaking that is Indian driving. The road was wide and smooth and apart from a water buffalo that had died standing up, uneventful. The unfortunate beast had been tied to a telegraph pole and had wound itself in tight before losing its footing and snapping its own neck.

⌐

A little more information about Coryate in India comes from Edward Terry, the parson attached to Thomas Roe's ambassadorial mission. Unfortunately Terry left nothing like the small goldmine of the Purchas notes, about which I had undergone a rather sheepish change of heart and for which I was now deeply grateful. With the exception of Coryate's letters, *Purchas his Pilgrims* contained the majority of the surviving first-hand material from Coryate. A luxury that was highlighted by Edward Terry's second-hand account, which, although it was generally accurate, did contain some howlers.

A Voyage to East India, published almost forty years after Coryate's death, confuses what Coryate had planned to do, with what he did. He went to Africa, Terry says, and to Egypt; although in reality Coryate did neither, having only talked of these places with Terry and included them as a possible route home in the letters.

Terry had some liking for the wandering *fakir* and his pioneering journey (Terry had simply sailed to India), yet disapproved of his approach. Fame was undoubtedly the reason for Coryate's journey, Terry said: 'hope of name and repute for the time to come did even feed and feast him for the time present.'

This must be seen in context of the time of course and also Coryate's own comment, that '... there hath itched a very burning desire in me ... to survey and contemplate some of the chiefest parts of this goodly fabric of the world ...' In the 17th century a man had to make the best of what chances came, especially a man from Coryate's modest social background.

But Coryate was not a straightforward person. His European trip and the *Crudities* had created a niche that he intended to occupy; travel had become his identity and his membership card to the elite group he had known at court. More than most of his contemporaries Coryate lacked the advantages of birth. Instead he relied on his character and on his own abilities; abilities that apparently included making a name for himself. It was a combination that allowed more modest men from better social backgrounds to look down their noses.

⤚

Joel Wellington Christie was in his fifties with black hair and a slightly anxious face. He lived at the end of a short line of mission houses in Surat's Mughalserai – 'Mughal camp' – district and I had come to speak to him because of his reputation as a historian. I hoped he could fill in the final gaps in Coryate's life.

Joel was passionate about history. He loved the intricacies of date and detail, the nuances of past lives and their interweaving with the present. He had collected scraps of information on Coryate for many years and knew of the confusion surrounding his grave. He had something to add, he said, because he thought there was a possibility that Coryate was buried at

Suvali. Or even that he was first buried there and his grave later moved. Similar things had happened once the English presence on the subcontinent was consolidated, although the evidence was slight. A mention in a Gujarati volume of history and a burial mound Joel remembered near the coast, but it was just possible.

'Edward Terry also described Coryate's grave in *A Voyage to East India*,' said Joel. 'He said that Coryate was buried at Suvali where there was already a burial plot.'

The problem, Joel went on, was that the land had never been protected. Cattle grazed there and many trees had grown, even in the years since he first saw the mound. To make matters worse the Tapti estuary changed almost every year. The grave could have been dug up, ploughed under or washed into the soupy brown river any time in the last 400 years. And Terry was an old man with an old man's memory when he wrote his book, 40 years after Coryate's death.

'They didn't keep records the way we do now,' Joel said. 'And Coryate would have fallen between two stools. He was not an employee of the East India Company and he wasn't under local jurisdiction. It was nobody's business to keep an eye on him, and so he came and went as he pleased. When he died he was no one's to claim.

'There are two sources that say he was buried in Surat and both might be better than Terry. They say the grave was near the Broach Gate.' The Broach Gate was one of four in Surat's medieval wall and was still in place during Coryate's time. 'Later that name was changed to Katargam Gate. The English cemetery is there now, an impressive place – you should go there and see the tombs, although I'm afraid they are not so well looked after these days. They don't get so much money there; it's just enough to pay the staff – and they are paid very little. Places like that are maintained by the Catholic Church or by the city authorities, and because no one visits them there is no income. They are forgotten places.'

Joel led me up a steep wooden staircase to a tiny upper floor of three rooms, two of which were full of books. Everything from Biblical commentaries in Hebrew to printers' manuals in Gujarati. Joel had been a printer before his retirement, he explained, and it told in this regimented enormity of paper.

'The two references are Herbert and Fryer,' he said, finger resting on a page. 'Thomas Herbert was part of a Persian ambassador's retinue on its way back to Persia in 1627.' He scanned the text. 'It says the ambassador was Sir Robert Sherley, and also that there was a rival Persian ambassador on the same ship, a man called Nagd Ali Begh. It says Begh committed suicide when the ship arrived in port, even though Islam expressly forbids this. Of course Christianity forbids it as well…'

He looked at the ceiling for a moment. 'Nagd Ali Begh had been in England in February 1626 as ambassador from Shah Abbas.' He said thoughtfully. 'Sir Robert Sherley was in the country at the same time, also claiming to have been sent on a similar mission and I think there was a quarrel between the two men. By order of King Charles I they were brought back in the East India Company's fleet [of 1627]. Nagd Ali Begh poisoned himself just before the ships reached the coast of India and his body was buried at Surat. It was thought that the tomb you have visited was his.'

Joel paused again.

'But I do not think this explanation is correct. There were some connections between Persia and India at the time, trading links and the like, but not too many high-level contacts. The problem becomes who paid for the monument to be built. Suicide is such a taboo in Islam that his death would have brought shame on his family. It would have been difficult for them to do much for him, especially as they were in another country.

'The other name is Dr John Fryer,' he said

returning to the book. 'He was a merchant who came to India in the 1670s. I think Herbert's information is probably better because he came to Surat ten years after Coryate died, though Fryer seems to confirm what Herbert says anyway. The grave was on the left hand side of the road outside Broach Gate.'

'But the cemetery is on the right hand side,' I said. I had a map of the city from my hotel and the cemetery was marked on it.

Joel smiled. 'There is nothing if not confusion when it comes to Thomas Coryate. In their favour both men report seeing the grave, where Terry does not. Terry was in Mandu at the time Coryate died.

'English trade was only just becoming established when Coryate came here and so there was no true cemetery at the time. Of course no one was buried inside the city limits then, not even the locals, it just wasn't done for fear of disease. By the time Fryer arrived in the mid-1600s there were a few English graves, as well as Dutch, French and also Armenian. Fryer's description puts Coryate's grave opposite what is now the English cemetery, and he also talks about the Persian ambassador.'

"The way [out of the city] is strewn with Muslim tombs, and one of especial note of the Persian ambassador who killed himself. Not far from whence on a small hill on the left hand of the road lies Thomas Coryate together with an Armenian, the graves lying east to west. From hence we passed over to the Dutch tombs.'

'I take "passed over" to mean crossed the road.' Joel said. 'Today that road is the main road north out of the city. Although on the other hand Suvali, where Terry puts the grave, is also outside the city. And Suvali was well known as an English location at the time. Passengers left their ships there and came to Surat by bullock cart because the estuary was so difficult to navigate. In the 16th century a Turkish ship took a week to sail from Suvali to Surat. And they could have chosen to put the Persian ambassador at Suvali because of his suicide ...'

We climbed back down the staircase and went through to Joel's minute porch facing the London Mission Church. In the quiet street a woman in a faded yellow sari was carrying firewood into her house and a child was playing with a tricycle. Neighbouring houses reduced the city to a background roar and replaced it with an air of outdoor domesticity.

'The first priest of the church, a man called Alexander Fyvie, fell out of that window,' Joel pointed to a small window high in the gable, 'and landed there.' He pointed to the concrete below, then swung his finger across the church courtyard. 'And that' – a solid piece of stonework beneath a dusty tree – 'is his tomb.' The luckless Fyvie's last journey had killed him too.

After *chai* in Joel's kitchen, made by his smiling wife, we walked around the church into a short alley-way. Down at the far end, an archway gave onto the bare red earth of a school playground separated from the glutinous Tapti River by a low wall.

'As far as I can make out,' Joel said, 'the English factory was here.' He stamped a foot.

'We excavated before the schools were built and made quite a few finds. Some English coins, pots, animal bones from food and other refuse. It proved that the area was once used by English merchants.'

He took a few steps, scanning the ground with his head bowed as though in meditation.

Coryate had spent a couple of fateful days here in December 1617 having walked from Mandu, prob-ably in around ten days. Once Roe had known of Coryate's plan to make for Surat he had asked Coryate to carry a letter addressed to the English consul in Aleppo. In the letter Roe asks the consul to receive Coryate well, as he was 'a very honest poor wretch' who had already travelled a great distance. Coryate came to hear of the phrase and was outraged. He was immediately back at court, singing for his supper and dancing for dessert. Coryate had been away from home for five years by this time, and in India for two (a year longer than Roe). He, not the reticent ambassador, was master here. He knew the highways and byways of northern India, had seen the shrines and the burning ghats, had been to the festivals and the holy river Ganges. He knew local customs of religion and daily practice and unlike Roe he spoke both of India's main languages *de jour*.

'Honest' certainly does describe Coryate, and as someone with a strong Puritan bent he made a virtue of being poor, but I for one still feel as Coryate did: *a little more respect, if you don't mind*. And he said as much, because it is recorded that Roe amended the letter to read more kindly before sealing it.

Prompted by this slight, and with King James' comment no doubt echoing in his ears, Coryate collected what few possession he travelled with and quit Mandu. He walked down from the ridge and onto the plain below, where he put his face to the setting sun and made for Surat and the English factory.

Somewhere beneath my feet was the ground Coryate trod 400 years ago. And somewhere too was the very spot where he died a few days after arriving.

The walk out to Katargam Gate was a melancholy one, through the chaotic city streets to where Surat once ended and where the foreign cemeteries still stand.

A high wall separates the road from the sagging dignity of the English graveyard; a square of parched land that was like a museum of funerary architecture. The largest mausoleum was that of Christopher and Sir George Oxenden, English brothers who died in 1659 and 1669 respectively. It was built on two floors and was the size of a house, with a cupola shaped like a pumpkin taking up the ground floor. Pressed up against this, one in each corner, were four *lingam*, the stylised phallus of Hindu mythology.

Another equally impressive tomb was that of Gerald Aungier, second governor of Bombay (Sir George Oxenden being the first) and president of the Surat factory. It was Aungier who had ejected the Portuguese when Bombay (anglicised from *Bom Baia*, 'good bay') came to Charles II as part of Catherine of Braganza's dowry.

The architecture was interesting because it represents a unique moment in colonial history. Within a few years European attitudes to the subcontinent would change. Graves would become more sombre and, significantly, more European. But just for a time all the grandeur England could muster, both to fend off other European powers and impress the Mughal Empire, was reflected in the magnificence of Surat's cemetery.

Unfortunately these great colonial statements also made it obvious that none of the tombs was Coryate's, although still I had to look for myself. It was part of my homage to Coryate, who hadn't taken anyone's word for the world; who hadn't been content to read the accounts of others or accept their opinions. If my trip was about anything it was about that self-centred empirical spirit – the spirit of travel.

So I walked into all the corners of the cemetery, examined the inscription on each stone and made notes on everything. The grass was surprisingly green, the north wall had dabs of moss and the ground level was a little higher at the back. But no Coryate. Nor even any overturned slabs to heave upright in the hope of finding his name.

Neither was the 'small hill' opposite the cemetery still there. The city that had ended at Katargam Gate 400 years ago, now ended two miles further out. For the last five years of his life no one knew where Thomas Coryate was. Four hundred years later and still no one knew.

What I finally managed to confirm by talking to Joel, and a couple of days later on a visit to Bombay's – now Mumbai's – musty libraries, was that while the monument may have been 'Tom Coryate's Tomb', it was not his grave.

What clinched it was a 19th-century gazetteer of the Bombay presidency which showed that the monument had been erected in 1697 to a man named Vaux, a former deputy-governor of Bombay. Vaux started his career as bookkeeper to Sir Josiah Childs and worked his way swiftly up through the ranks. He became first a merchant in his own right, then judge, then deputy-governor. Then after an unrecorded incident Vaux was suddenly suspended from duty, and, although nothing was ever proved, the rumour was that he was a French spy. Depending on whom you believed he was either the perpetrator or victim of an intrigue which, either way, saw off a promising career. A year later out boating with his wife on the Tapti there was an accident and they were pitched into the river. The general social distaste for swimming as unseemly, even as something resembling a form of manual labour, meant it was unlikely either could swim, and this coupled with the clothing of the day ensured they didn't survive.

From other construction expenses of the day a rough

estimate of the monument's cost might be around £150 (approximately £18,000 at today's prices). It seems very unlikely that anyone would spend such an amount on Thomas Coryate, the 'penniless fakir' who made a virtue of being broke, boasted of making it from Aleppo to Ajmer on £3 (including what was stolen) and who died in possession of perhaps as little as £10. It is equally unlikely that anyone else put up such a sum on Coryate's behalf, and as Joel had ruled out the Persian ambassador it seems that Vaux, The Company man, is the true owner of Coryate's tomb.

Sad indeed that a man like Coryate who craved recognition should have suffered such an end. But then that too was a pioneering death. The first modern traveller dying the first traveller's death abroad.

Epilogue

On the morning I flew home – undoing in nine hours what had taken nine months to do – I went back to 'Tom Coryate's Tomb'. I was looking for the intangible something I had come to associate with Coryate and I still hoped the tomb could provide it; a symbol of the magic and mystique of travel that was now synonymous with his name.

But already it felt as though I was visiting an alien place. The weather was colder, the sky was overcast and eventually it rained. A dark shadow dropped down the building soaking up the colours, turning the monument into a blot in the greenery. It became a small drab corner of the world.

I stood in the bush gazing silently, taking leave, feeling somehow betrayed, as if a lover's purity had been found wanting. I had expected the tomb to encapsulate the man I now knew through travel; expected it to acknowledge the hardships he had faced on his walk through an unknown world to this particular end of the Earth. Coryate had made a significant contribution to modern culture and I wanted the tomb that bore his name to reflect this.

Even despite the lack of recognition the tomb was still a beautiful, even a poignant place. But in the rain that afternoon I came to realise that Coryate's spirit was not to be found in anything physical. What he represented was now present in travel itself, and in my version of his journey, which brought me to this spot. A journey that had already become more than a combination of the people I had met and the places I had seen. My trip in Coryate's footsteps was no longer something I had done. The journey had become a new place in itself. A new country created by travel.

Bibliography

Barbour, Richmond, *Before Orientalism* (Cambridge University Press, Cambridge: 2003).

Beattie, Andrew, and Timothy Pepper, *Syria* (Rough Guides, London: 1998).

Bernier, François, and Archibald Constable (trans.), Vincent A Smith (ed.) *Travels in the Mogul Empire* (Low Price Publications, New Delhi: 1999).

Brennan, Michael G (ed.), *The Origins of the Grand Tour* (Hakluyt Society, London: 2004).

Burns, Ross, *Monuments of Syria* (I B Taurus, London: 1992).

Coryate, Thomas, *Coryat's Crudities* (Maclehose, Glasgow: 1905).

Cravan, Roy. *Indian Art* (Thames and Hudson, London: 1997).

Donne, John. *The Complete English Poems* (Penguin, London: 1971).

Eraly, Abraham, *The Mughal Throne* (Weidenfeld and Nicolson, London: 2003).

Foster, William (ed.), *Early Travels in India* (Oriental Books Reprint Corp, New Delhi: 1985)

Foster, William, *The Embassy of Sir Thomas Roe to India* (Munshiram Manoharlal, New Delhi: 1990).

Hakluyt, Richard, Laurence Irving (ed.), *Hakluyt's Voyages* (William Heinemann, London: 1927).

Hillenbrand, Robert, *Islamic Architecture* (Edinburgh University Press, Edinburgh: 1994).

Keay, John *India: a History* (Harper Collins, London: 2000).

Khomeini, Ayatollah, *Sayings of Ayatollah Khomeini* (Bantam Books, New York: 1980).

Knapp, Grace H (ed.), *The Tragedy of Bitlis* (Taderon Press, Reading: 2002).

Knolles, Richard, *The Generall Historie of the Turkes* (London: 1603).

Kwon, Paul P W, *From Cairo to Paris* (JM Media, Seoul: 2004).

Lewis, Bernard, *The Assassins* (Phoenix, London: 1967).

Mitchell, Colin Paul, *Sir Thomas Roe and the Mughal Empire* (Area Study Centre for Europe, Karachi: 2000).

Moore, Tim, *Continental Drifter* (Abacus, London: 2002).

Moraes, Dom, and Sarayu Srivatsa, *The Long Strider* (Penguin Books India, New Delhi: 2003).

Purchas, Samuel, *Purchas His Pilgrims* (London: 1625).

Rogers, Alexander (trans.), Henry Beveridge (ed.), *The Memoirs of Jahangir* (Low Price Publications, New Delhi: 1999).

Said, Edward, *Orientalism* (Penguin, London: 2003).

Shayesteh, Mahmoud Reza, and Mansour Ghassemi, *Esfahan A Tiny Earthly Paradise* (Mahmoud Reza Shayesteh, Esfahan: 2004).

Strachan, Michael, *The Life and Adventures of Thomas Coryate* (Oxford University Press, Oxford: 1962).

Wright, Arnold (ed.), *Early English Adventurers in the East* (Sang-e-Meel Publications, Lahore: 2000).

Khy

Tripoli
Antoom
Tabriz
Ardebil
Machenet

Mosul
Oroomia
L. Ouroumia
Reshd
Jah Jerm
Jor

Beirout
Damascus
Palmyra
Ana
R. Shabrazour
Luijan
Hamadan
Casbin
TEHERAN
Saree
Astrabad

Jericho
Dead Sea
Hit
Euphrates
R. Kermanshah
Bagdad
Koom
KHORAS

Barrae
el Sham
Billah
Deophoul
Kasban
Ispahan
Tubbus
Khaff
Toot

El Hassa
Akaba
Desert
Shica
Plain of El Hamele
or Al Daina
Shuster
Nain
Yezd
Neh

Moveleh
Teboude
Istabel Anton
Feid
Ras
Amizeh
R E
Bussora
Endian
Babahan
Moorgheib
Naswarabad

Yembo
Medina
Shakra
Derayeh
Karatnin
Lahsa
Jemama
R. Aftan
Busheer
Taren
Lar
Shiraz
Derabgherd
Kerman
Hubbees

KERMAN
Gamberoon
Kishma
Minab
Serek
Basra

Meldca
Serrain
Niab
Nedsjeran
Musseldon
Rostak
Oman
Churbar
Muskat
Kothant

ARABIAN GULF or RED SEA
Giorrash
Saade
Desert of Akhaf
Doan
Ganco
Ras al Had

Lobeya
Chamir
Sana
Rodda
Kataba
Damar
Dofor
Plain
of Mahra
Shibam
Massera

Mokha
Perim I.
Bab el Mandeb
Aden
C. South East
C. Kartak
Ras Morbat
Soorva Moorva Bay
Sungra Bay
Ras Madrake

HADHAR EL MOUT

AFRICA
C. Guardafui
Ras Bar
Socotra

GULF OF PERSIA

ARABIA
NEDJED
HEDJAZ
YEMEN